XENOPHON'S

SYMPOSIUM

With Notes

BY

SAMUEL ROSS WINANS, Ph.D.

PROFESSOR OF GREEK IN PRINCETON UNIVERSITY

καὶ γὰρ παίζων οὐδὲν ἧττον ἢ σπουδάζων ἐλυσιτέλει τοῖς συνδιατρίβουσιν. — MEM. SOCR. IV. i. 1.

Boston

ALLYN AND BACON

1896

UNIVERSITY PRESS:
JOHN WILSON AND SON, CAMBRIDGE.

PREFACE.

◆

XENOPHON was both a prolific and a versatile writer. He had the good fortune in every instance to choose subjects of peculiar historical interest. Genius cannot be claimed for him : he had the constructive faculty, but not an imagination of the highest, poetic type. So too he better illustrates in his own life and character the practical side of the Socratic philosophy than he succeeds in expounding its dialectic.

Xenophon's productions, nevertheless, after their kind possess great merit ; while in an historical aspect some of them are wholly unique and incomparably valuable. His style is a model for narrative prose : simple and direct, not stilted or verbose, and when in his best vein, sprightly and charming. He is especially remarkable for the varied orders of composition which he essays ; some of which he originated.

Thus he has left us that matchless narrative of the fortunes of the ten thousand Greeks in their fateful march into and out of the Persian empire ; a history of Greek affairs, somewhat biased, it is true, but covering an important period, for which he is quite the sole

authority ; the first European romance, in which he
writes with a purpose, to set forth ideal views on poli-
tics and ethics ; a panegyric on his favorite hero,
Agesilaus ; several political tracts also ; treatises on
hunting and horsemanship ; and most valuable of all,
the first volume of memoirs that has come down to
us, his recollections of Socrates, wherein with loving
hand he gives faithful life-sketches of the noble man
and pure teacher, just as he lived and walked among
men.

Xenophon was also among the first to employ the
philosophical dialogue, which Plato carried to such
perfection ; Xenophon too employing Socrates as pro-
tagonist in presenting his own theories on household
and agricultural management.

And finally he has the credit of having composed
the earliest formal prose account of a banquet.

The object of the SYMPOSIUM is clearly indicated
in its opening statement.   It is designed as an after-
piece to the *Memorabilia :* in it Xenophon would present more distinctively one special aspect of a great
man's character, his sociability ; his geniality and
boundless good humor ; how gracefully he could in-
termingle serious reflections, and how beneath all his
pleasantry there lurked an earnest, moral purpose.
At the same time he undoubtedly designs to give an
ideal sketch of a dinner party, where the guests are
men of culture, but at the same time men of flesh
and blood, who talk and act just as they might in real
life.

And not inconsistent with these general aims, he manages to put Socrates on record as to his views on love and certain all too prevalent vices of the day. Xenophon's motive may thus have been a triple one.

The plot itself is very simple. The order and relation of the separate events, the balance of the parts, and the management of the details, are studied with as much care as in a drama, and show no little artistic skill. Callias, a wealthy Athenian, gives a supper in honor of a young friend, Autolycus, who has gained a victory in the pancratium at the public games. Socrates and a few of his followers are present by special personal invitation of the host, given as he meets them that same day. The course of events is sufficiently outlined by the summaries interspersed through the text. A buffoon, and a showman with his little troupe of dancers, trick-performers and musicians, are characteristically introduced. Little is said of the dishes or the dinner proper. The various amusements are described, and we are supposed to have a complete report of their merry table-talk. Socrates is made the central figure, but not so obtrusively as to overshadow the other characters. He calms every incipient quarrel, guides the conversation into the most interesting channels, and charms all by his genial manners and his often audacious but always innocent wit. Yet we have no less distinct portraits of Hermogenes with his retiring disposition and almost morbid piety, or of Niceratus, the close-fisted capitalist, with his verse of scripture ready for every occasion, or of Antisthenes, that irrepressible disputant and shrewd sophist.

The genuineness of this work has rarely been called in question. The date of its composition cannot be determined with precision. It evidently was composed after the *Memorabilia*, hence in that fruitful period of literary labor which ensued upon Xenophon's retirement to Scillus; therefore about 390 B.C., not later, however, than 385.

The date assigned to the banquet, as determined by that of the event which gave it occasion, is 421 B.C. There are few, if any, glaring anachronisms in the sketch, certainly not more than may be readily conceded one who pictures an ideal scene. For, natural and life-like as the affair is, no one would now hold that it is an accurate description of an actual supper. Its truthfulness is poetical rather than historical. This view is strengthened, if proof were needed, by the fact that Xenophon according to the latest conclusions as to his age was too young — about 10 — to take part in such an affair. Hence the introductory statement, 'at which I was present,' must be interpreted as the novelist's license, — not, unnatural in the author of the *Cyropædia*. The clumsiness of indirect discourse is avoided, and the narrative gains in vividness.

Plato's *Symposium* was probably written later than Xenophon's. The marked contrasts in the details of these works need not, as some have thought, argue any personal animosity or even literary rivalry be-

tween the authors. Plato's work is characterized by
a matchless elegance of diction, by a rich, pervasive
humor of a high, intellectual style, and by its philosophical cast and *motif*. Superb as a work of art, it
is idealized quite away from the possibilities of actual
life.

Xenophon's piece, on the other hand, is less pre-
tentious : in a simple, graceful style it gives a pleasant
and trustworthy picture from old Greek life. Its natu-
ralness constitutes at once its value and its charm.
The estimate of it from ancient times down has been
uniformly appreciative. Mure's exceptional adverse
position is taken not only from the exacting stand-
point of modern ethics, but also with a total miscon-
ception of the true spirit of the work. Mahaffy, whose
special researches make him a more competent critic,
shows more discrimination and gives a sounder judgment. In a course of classical reading the Symposium according to its original design makes a
delightful after-piece to the *Memorabilia*. Indepen-
dently it has great value : as a source of information
on ancient life ; for the insight into the idiom and
spirit of the language which its conversational style
affords the student ; and not less for the lively interest and sympathy with the personality of the Greeks
which this intimate introduction to their social life
arouses, — an interest which naturally extends itself
to the higher forms of their literature.

The text is based on the recension of Schenkl
(Berlin, 1876): in not a few cases, however, of arbi-

trary and gratuitous alteration the Mss. readings have
been restored, generally thus in agreement with the
texts of Sauppe (Leip., 1866) and L. Dindorf (Leip.,
1876). Chapter VIII has been omitted, an episode
quite unessential, and introducing matters not suited
to the plan and purpose of the present volume. The
few other slight omissions, it is hoped, will be considered judicious and sufficient.

The following auxiliaries are suggested to students.
For a popular, intelligible, and appreciative exposi-
tion of Socrates' worth as a thinker and teacher, the
chapter "Socrates" in John Stuart Blackie's *Four
Phases of Morals* is unsurpassed. The volume
Xenophon in the series "Ancient Classics for English
Readers," gives a racy sketch of Xenophon's career
and an entertaining outline of his works; for a brief
general account of him, especially as Socrates' biogra-
pher, see Introduction to author's edition of the
Memorabilia; for a glance at his place in Greek literature, Jebb's *Primer;* for the same with critical esti-
mates, Mahaffy's *Greek Literature*, Vol. II.

For fuller information on ancient manners and customs, original sources are: Plato's *Symposium*, —
already mentioned; Plutarch's *Symposium of Seven
Sages* and his *Symposiacs*, — tedious and pedantic;
Lucian's *Symposium, or Lapithae*, — a travesty; Athenæus' *Deipnosophists*, — a thesaurus of facts respect-
ing the externals of banquets, food, wines, and the
like, but presented with little system or artistic skill,
and consequently dull. Of modern treatises, these

and similar are valuable : Becker's *Charicles;* St. John's *Ancient Greeks;* Felton's *Lectures,* Vol. I., second course, "The Life of Greece"; Guhl and Koner, *Life of the Greeks and Romans;* Mahaffy's *Primer of Old Greek Life,* and his essays on *Social Life in Greece;* together with the Histories and special dictionaries.

PRINCETON, N. J.,
April, 1881.

IN this edition of the SYMPOSIUM errors of the press have been corrected, and a few other slight changes made. To the above list of auxiliaries may now be added the recent very complete edition of this piece by G. F. Rettig (Leipzig, 1881).

S. R. W.

PRINCETON,
January, 1883.

ΞΕΝΟΦΩΝΤΟΣ

ΣΥΜΠΟΣΙΟΝ.

—•◦•—

Παίζειν ἐν τῷ βίῳ καὶ περὶ μηδὲν
ἁπλῶς σπουδάζειν. — Simonides : frag. 192.

CHAPTER I.

The theme, the occasion, and the guests.

Ἀλλ᾽ ἐμοὶ δοκεῖ τῶν καλῶν κἀγαθῶν ἀν- 1
δρῶν ἔργα οὐ μόνον τὰ μετὰ σπουδῆς
πραττόμενα ἀξιομνημόνευτα εἶναι, ἀλλὰ καὶ
τὰ ἐν ταῖς παιδιαῖς. οἷς δὲ παραγενόμενος
ταῦτα γιγνώσκω δηλῶσαι βούλομαι.

Ἦν μὲν γὰρ Παναθηναίων τῶν μεγάλων 2
ἱπποδρομία, Καλλίας δὲ ὁ Ἱππονίκου ἐρῶν
ἐτύγχανεν Αὐτολύκου παιδὸς ὄντος, καὶ νε-
νικηκότα αὐτὸν παγκράτιον ἧκεν ἄγων ἐπὶ
τὴν θέαν. ὡς δὲ ἡ ἱπποδρομία ἔληξεν, ἔχων
τόν τε Αὐτόλυκον καὶ τὸν πατέρα αὐτοῦ
ἀπῄει εἰς τὴν ἐν Πειραιεῖ οἰκίαν· συνείπετο
δὲ αὐτῷ καὶ Νικήρατος. ἰδὼν δὲ ὁμοῦ ὄντας 3
Σωκράτην τε καὶ Κριτόβουλον καὶ Ἑρμο-
γένην καὶ Ἀντισθένην καὶ Χαρμίδην, τοῖς
μὲν ἀμφ᾽ Αὐτόλυκον ἡγεῖσθαί τινα ἔταξεν,
αὐτὸς δὲ προσῆλθε τοῖς ἀμφὶ Σωκράτην,

4 καὶ εἶπεν, Εἰς καλόν γε ὑμῖν συντετύχηκα·
ἑστιᾶν γὰρ μέλλω Αὐτόλυκον καὶ τὸν πατέρα αὐτοῦ. οἶμαι οὖν πολὺ ἂν τὴν κατα-
σκευήν μοι λαμπροτέραν φανῆναι, εἰ ἀνδράσιν
ἐκκεκαθαρμένοις τὰς ψυχὰς ὥσπερ ὑμῖν ὁ
ἀνδρὼν κεκοσμημένος εἴη μᾶλλον ἢ εἰ στρα-
5 τηγοῖς καὶ ἱππάρχοις καὶ σπουδαρχίαις. καὶ
ὁ Σωκράτης εἶπεν, Ἀεὶ σὺ ἐπισκώπτεις ἡμᾶς
καταφρονῶν, ὅτι σὺ μὲν Πρωταγόρᾳ τε
πολὺ ἀργύριον δέδωκας ἐπὶ σοφίᾳ καὶ Γορ-
γίᾳ καὶ Προδίκῳ καὶ ἄλλοις πολλοῖς, ἡμᾶς
δ᾽ ὁρᾷς αὐτουργούς τινας τῆς φιλοσοφίας
6 ὄντας. καὶ ὁ Καλλίας, Καὶ πρόσθεν μέν
γε, ἔφη, ἀπεκρυπτόμην ὑμᾶς ἔχων πολλὰ
καὶ σοφὰ λέγειν, νῦν δέ, ἐὰν παρ᾽ ἐμοὶ ἦτε,
ἐπιδείξω ὑμῖν ἐμαυτὸν πάνυ πολλῆς σπουδῆς
7 ἄξιον ὄντα. οἱ οὖν ἀμφὶ τὸν Σωκράτην
πρῶτον μέν, ὥσπερ εἰκὸς ἦν, ἐπαινοῦντες
τὴν κλῆσιν οὐχ ὑπισχνοῦντο συνδειπνήσειν·
ὡς δὲ πάνυ ἀχθόμενος φανερὸς ἦν, εἰ μὴ
ἕψοιντο, συνηκολούθησαν. ἔπειτα δὲ αὐτῷ οἱ
μὲν γυμνασάμενοι καὶ χρισάμενοι, οἱ δὲ καὶ
8 λουσάμενοι παρῆλθον. Αὐτόλυκος μὲν οὖν
παρὰ τὸν πατέρα ἐκαθέζετο, οἱ δ᾽ ἄλλοι
ὥσπερ εἰκὸς κατεκλίθησαν.

[*With these beauty-loving Greeks the handsome Autolycus at once becomes the cynosure of all eyes. The
company at the outset feel a certain constraint.*]

Entrance of a parasite buffoon, and the discomfiture of
his wit.

Ἐκεῖνοι μὲν οὖν σιωπῇ ἐδείπνουν, ὥσπερ 11
τοῦτο ἐπιτεταγμένον αὐτοῖς ὑπὸ κρείττονός
τινος. Φίλιππος δ᾽ ὁ γελωτοποιὸς κρούσας
τὴν θύραν εἶπε τῷ ὑπακούσαντι εἰσαγγεῖλαι
ὅστις τε εἴη καὶ διότι κατάγεσθαι βούλοιτο·
συνεσκευασμένος δὲ παρεῖναι ἔφη πάντα τὰ
ἐπιτήδεια ὥστε δειπνεῖν τἀλλότρια, καὶ τὸν
παῖδα δὲ ἔφη πάνυ πιέζεσθαι διά τε τὸ φέρειν μηδὲν καὶ διὰ τὸ ἀνάριστον εἶναι. ὁ 12
οὖν Καλλίας ἀκούσας ταῦτα εἶπεν, Ἀλλὰ
μέντοι, ὦ ἄνδρες, αἰσχρὸν στέγης γε φθονῆ-
σαι· εἰσίτω οὖν. καὶ ἅμα ἀπέβλεψεν εἰς τὸν
Αὐτόλυκον, δῆλον ὅτι ἐπισκοπῶν τί ἐκείνῳ
δόξειε τὸ σκῶμμα εἶναι. ὁ δὲ στὰς ἐπὶ τῷ 13
ἀνδρῶνι ἔνθα τὸ δεῖπνον ἦν εἶπεν, Ὅτι μὲν
γελωτοποιός εἰμι ἴστε πάντες· ἥκω δὲ προθύμως νομίσας γελοιότερον εἶναι τὸ ἄκλητον
ἢ τὸ κεκλημένον ἐλθεῖν ἐπὶ τὸ δεῖπνον. Κα-
τακλίνου τοίνυν, ἔφη ὁ Καλλίας. καὶ γὰρ οἱ
παρόντες σπουδῆς μέν, ὡς ὁρᾷς, μεστοί, γέλωτος δὲ ἴσως ἐνδεέστεροι. δειπνούντων δὲ 14
αὐτῶν ὁ Φίλιππος γελοῖόν τι εὐθὺς ἐπεχείρει
λέγειν, ἵνα δὴ ἐπιτελοίη ὧνπερ ἕνεκα ἐκα-
λεῖτο ἑκάστοτε ἐπὶ τὰ δεῖπνα. ὡς δ᾽ οὐκ
ἐκίνησε γέλωτα, τότε μὲν ἀχθεσθεὶς φανερὸς
ἐγένετο. αὖθις δ᾽ ὀλίγον ὕστερον ἄλλο τι

γελοῖον ἐβούλετο λέγειν. ὡς δὲ οὐδὲ τότε
ἐγέλασαν ἐπ᾿ αὐτῷ, ἐν τῷ μεταξὺ παυσάμε-
νος τοῦ δείπνου συγκαλυψάμενος κατέκειτο.
15 καὶ ὁ Καλλίας, Τί τοῦτ᾿, ἔφη, ὦ Φίλιππε ;
ἀλλ᾿ ἢ ὀδύνη σε εἴληφε ; καὶ ὃς ἀναστενάξας
εἶπε, Ναὶ μὰ Δί᾿, ἔφη, ὦ Καλλία, μεγάλη
γε· ἐπεὶ γὰρ γέλως ἐξ ἀνθρώπων ἀπόλω-
λεν, ἔρρει τὰ ἐμὰ πράγματα. πρόσθεν μὲν
γὰρ τούτου ἕνεκα ἐκαλούμην ἐπὶ τὰ δεῖπνα,
ἵνα εὐφραίνοιντο οἱ συνόντες δι᾿ ἐμὲ γελῶν-
τες· νῦν δὲ τίνος ἕνεκα καὶ καλεῖ μέ τις ;
οὔτε γὰρ ἔγωγε σπουδάσαι ἂν δυναίμην μᾶλλον ἤπερ ἀθάνατος γενέσθαι, οὔτε μὴν ὡς
ἀντικληθησόμενος καλεῖ μέ τις, ἐπεὶ πάντες
ἴσασιν ὅτι ἀρχὴν οὐδὲ νομίζεται εἰς τὴν ἐμὴν
οἰκίαν δεῖπνον εἰσφέρεσθαι. καὶ ἅμα λέγων
ταῦτα ἀπεμύττετό τε καὶ τῇ φωνῇ σαφῶς
16 κλαίειν ἐφαίνετο. πάντες μὲν οὖν παρεμυ-
θοῦντό τε αὐτὸν ὡς αὖθις γελασόμενοι καὶ
δειπνεῖν ἐκέλευον, Κριτόβουλος δὲ καὶ ἐξε-
κάγχασεν ἐπὶ τῷ οἰκτισμῷ αὐτοῦ. ὁ δ᾿ ὡς
ᾔσθετο τοῦ γέλωτος, ἀνεκαλύψατό τε καὶ τῇ
ψυχῇ παρακελευσάμενος θαρρεῖν, ὅτι ἔσονται
συμβολαί, πάλιν ἐδείπνει.

CHAPTER II.

The κῶμος, or revel. Enter a minstrel troupe. Music, dancing, etc. Socrates' merry talk: first, of odors — literal
and figurative.

Ὡς δ' ἀφῃρέθησαν αἱ τράπεζαι καὶ ἔσπει- 1
σάν τε καὶ ἐπαιάνισαν, ἔρχεται αὐτοῖς ἐπὶ
κῶμον Συρακόσιός τις ἄνθρωπος, ἔχων τε
αὐλητρίδα ἀγαθὴν καὶ ὀρχηστρίδα τῶν τὰ
θαύματα δυναμένων ποιεῖν, καὶ παῖδα πάνυ
γε ὡραῖον καὶ πάνυ καλῶς κιθαρίζοντα καὶ
ὀρχούμενον. ταῦτα δὲ καὶ ἐπιδεικνὺς ὡς ἐν
θαύματι ἀργύριον ἐλάμβανεν. ἐπεὶ δὲ αὐτοῖς 2
ἡ αὐλητρὶς μὲν ηὔλησεν, ὁ δὲ παῖς ἐκιθάρισε,
καὶ ἐδόκουν μάλα ἀμφότεροι ἱκανῶς εὐφραίνειν, εἶπεν ὁ Σωκράτης, Νὴ Δί', ὦ Καλλία,
τελέως ἡμᾶς ἑστιᾷς. οὐ γὰρ μόνον δεῖπνον
ἄμεμπτον παρέθηκας, ἀλλὰ καὶ θεάματα καὶ
ἀκροάματα ἥδιστα παρέχεις. καὶ ὃς ἔφη, Τί 3
οὖν εἰ καὶ μύρον τις ἡμῖν ἐνέγκοι, ἵνα καὶ
εὐωδίᾳ ἑστιώμεθα; Μηδαμῶς, ἔφη ὁ Σωκράτης.
ὥσπερ γάρ τοι ἐσθὴς ἄλλη μὲν γυναικί, ἄλλη
δὲ ἀνδρὶ καλή, οὕτω καὶ ὀσμὴ ἄλλη μὲν ἀν-
δρί, ἄλλη δὲ γυναικὶ πρέπει. καὶ γὰρ ἀνδρὸς
μὲν δήπου ἕνεκα ἀνὴρ οὐδεὶς μύρῳ χρίεται.
αἱ μέντοι γυναῖκες ἄλλως τε καὶ ἢν νύμφαι
τύχωσιν οὖσαι, ὥσπερ ἡ Νικηράτου τοῦδε καὶ
ἡ Κριτοβούλου, μύρου μὲν τί καὶ προσδέον-

χειν, ῥᾳδίως τοῖς γε ἄλλοις ἵπποις χρήσε-
σθαι. κἀγὼ δὴ βουλόμενος ἀνθρώποις χρῆσθαι
καὶ ὁμιλεῖν ταύτην κέκτημαι, εὖ εἰδὼς ὅτι εἰ
ταύτην ὑποίσω, ῥᾳδίως τοῖς γε ἄλλοις ἅπασιν
ἀνθρώποις συνέσομαι. καὶ οὗτος μὲν δὴ ὁ
λόγος οὐκ ἄπο τοῦ σκοποῦ ἔδοξεν εἰρῆσθαι.

Vaulting over swords.   Courage teachable.

11   Μετὰ δὲ τοῦτο κύκλος εἰσηνέχθη περίμε-
στος ξιφῶν ὀρθῶν. εἰς οὖν ταῦτα ἡ ὀρχη-
στρὶς ἐκυβίστα τε καὶ ἐξεκυβίστα ὑπὲρ αὐτῶν. ὥστε οἱ μὲν θεώμενοι ἐφοβοῦντο μή τι
πάθῃ, ἡ δὲ θαρρούντως τε καὶ ἀσφαλῶς ταῦτα
12 διεπράττετο. καὶ ὁ Σωκράτης καλέσας τὸν
Ἀντισθένην εἶπεν, Οὗτοι τούς γε θεωμένους
τάδε ἀντιλέξειν ἔτι οἴομαι ὡς οὐχὶ καὶ ἡ
ἀνδρεία διδακτόν, ὁπότε αὕτη καίπερ γυνὴ
13 οὖσα οὕτω τολμηρῶς εἰς τὰ ξίφη ἵεται. καὶ
ὁ Ἀντισθένης εἶπεν, Ἆρ' οὖν καὶ τῷδε τῷ
Συρακοσίῳ κράτιστον ἐπιδείξαντι τῇ πόλει
τὴν ὀρχηστρίδα εἰπεῖν, ἐὰν διδῶσιν αὐτῷ
Ἀθηναῖοι χρήματα, ποιήσειν πάντας Ἀθηναί-
14 ους τολμᾶν ὁμόσε ταῖς λόγχαις ἰέναι; καὶ ὁ
Φίλιππος, Νὴ Δί', ἔφη, καὶ μὴν ἔγωγε ἡδέως
ἂν θεῴμην Πείσανδρον τὸν δημηγόρον μανθά-
νοντα κυβιστᾶν εἰς τὰς μαχαίρας, ὃς νῦν διὰ
τὸ μὴ δύνασθαι λόγχαις ἀντιβλέπειν οὐδὲ
συστρατεύεσθαι ἐθέλει.

The beauty of dancing, and its value as exercise.

Ἐκ τούτου ὁ παῖς ὠρχήσατο. καὶ ὁ Σω- 15
κράτης εἶπεν, Εἴδετ᾽, ἔφη, ὡς καλὸς ὁ παῖς
ὢν ὅμως σὺν τοῖς σχήμασιν ἔτι καλλίων φαί-
νεται ἢ ὅταν ἡσυχίαν ἔχῃ; καὶ ὁ Χαρμίδης
εἶπεν, Ἐπαινοῦντι ἔοικας τὸν ὀρχηστοδιδά-
σκαλον. Ναὶ μὰ τὸν Δί᾽, ἔφη ὁ Σωκράτης· 16
καὶ γὰρ ἄλλο τι προσενενόησα, ὅτι οὐδὲν
ἀργὸν τοῦ σώματος ἐν τῇ ὀρχήσει ἦν, ἀλλ᾽
ἅμα καὶ τράχηλος καὶ σκέλη καὶ χεῖρες ἐγυ-
μνάζοντο, ὥσπερ χρὴ ὀρχεῖσθαι τὸν μέλλοντα
εὐφορώτερον τὸ σῶμα ἕξειν. καὶ ἐγὼ μέν,
ἔφη, πάνυ ἂν ἡδέως, ὦ Συρακόσιε, μάθοιμι
τὰ σχήματα παρὰ σοῦ. καὶ ὅς, Τί οὖν
χρήσει αὐτοῖς; ἔφη. Ὀρχήσομαι νὴ Δία. 17
ἐνταῦθα δὴ ἐγέλασαν ἅπαντες. καὶ ὁ Σωκράτης μάλα ἐσπουδακότι τῷ προσώπῳ, Γελᾶτε,
ἔφη, ἐπ᾽ ἐμοί; πότερον ἐπὶ τούτῳ εἰ βούλομαι γυμναζόμενος μᾶλλον ὑγιαίνειν ἢ εἰ ἥδιον
ἐσθίειν καὶ καθεύδειν ἢ εἰ τοιούτων γυμνα-
σίων ἐπιθυμῶ, μὴ ὥσπερ οἱ δολιχοδρόμοι τὰ
σκέλη μὲν παχύνονται, τοὺς ὤμους δὲ λεπτύνονται, μηδ᾽ ὥσπερ οἱ πύκται τοὺς μὲν ὤμους
παχύνονται, τὰ δὲ σκέλη λεπτύνονται, ἀλλὰ
παντὶ διαπονῶν τῷ σώματι πᾶν ἰσόρροπον
ποιεῖν; ἢ ἐπ᾽ ἐκείνῳ γελᾶτε ὅτι οὐ δεήσει με 18
συγγυμναστὴν ζητεῖν, οὐδ᾽ ἐν ὄχλῳ πρεσβύ-

τὴν ὄντα ἀποδύσεσθαι, ἀλλ' ἀρκέσει μοι οἶκος
ἑπτάκλινος, ὥσπερ καὶ νῦν τῷδε τῷ παιδὶ
ἤρκεσε τόδε τὸ οἴκημα ἐνιδρῶσαι, καὶ χειμῶ-
νος μὲν ἐν στέγῃ γυμνάσομαι, ὅταν δὲ ἄγαν
19 καῦμα ᾖ, ἐν σκιᾷ; ἢ τόδε γελᾶτε, εἰ μείζω
τοῦ καιροῦ τὴν γαστέρα ἔχων μετριωτέραν
βούλομαι ποιῆσαι αὐτήν; ἢ οὐκ ἴστε ὅτι
ἔναγχος ἕωθεν Χαρμίδης οὑτοσὶ κατέλαβέ με
ὀρχούμενον; Ναὶ μὰ τὸν Δί', ἔφη ὁ Χαρμί-
δης· καὶ τὸ μέν γε πρῶτον ἐξεπλάγην καὶ
ἔδεισα μὴ μαίνοιο· ἐπεὶ δέ σου ἤκουσα ὅμοια
οἷς νῦν λέγεις, καὶ αὐτὸς ἐλθὼν οἴκαδε ὠρχού-
μην μὲν οὔ, οὐ γὰρ πώποτε τοῦτ' ἔμαθον,
20 ἐχειρονόμουν δέ· ταῦτα γὰρ ἠπιστάμην. Νὴ
Δί', ἔφη ὁ Φίλιππος, καὶ γὰρ οὖν οὕτω τὰ
σκέλη τοῖς ὤμοις φαίνει ἰσοφόρα ἔχειν ὥστε
δοκεῖς ἐμοί, κἂν εἰ τοῖς ἀγορανόμοις ἀφι-
στῷης ὥσπερ ἄρτους τὰ κάτω πρὸς τὰ ἄνω,
ἀζήμιος ἂν γενέσθαι. καὶ ὁ Καλλίας εἶπεν,
Ὦ Σώκρατες, ἐμὲ μὲν παρακάλει, ὅταν μέλ-
λῃς μανθάνειν ὀρχεῖσθαι, ἵνα σοι ἀντιστοιχῶ
τε καὶ συμμανθάνω.

The antics of the jester. Wine is served. Socrates' happy
suggestion for moderation.

21 Ἄγε δή, ἔφη ὁ Φίλιππος, καὶ ἐμοὶ αὐλη-
σάτω, ἵνα καὶ ἐγὼ ὀρχήσωμαι. ἐπειδὴ δ'
ἀνέστη, διῆλθε μιμούμενος τήν τε τοῦ παιδὸς

καὶ τὴν τῆς παιδὸς ὄρχησιν. καὶ πρῶτον μὲν 22
ὅτι ἐπήνεσαν ὡς ὁ παῖς σὺν τοῖς σχήμασιν
ἔτι καλλίων ἐφαίνετο, ἀνταπέδειξεν ὅ τι κι-
νοίη τοῦ σώματος ἅπαν τῆς φύσεως γελοιό-
τερον· ὅτι δ᾽ ἡ παῖς εἰς τοὔπισθεν καμπτο-
μένη τροχοὺς ἐμιμεῖτο, ἐκεῖνος ταῦτα εἰς τὸ
ἔμπροσθεν ἐπικύπτων μιμεῖσθαι τροχοὺς ἐπει-
ρᾶτο. τέλος δ᾽ ὅτι τὸν παῖδ᾽ ἐπήνουν ὡς ἐν
τῇ ὀρχήσει ἅπαν τὸ σῶμα γυμνάζοι, κελεύ-
σας τὴν αὐλητρίδα θάττονα ῥυθμὸν ἐπάγειν
ἵει ἅμα πάντα καὶ σκέλη καὶ χεῖρας καὶ κε-
φαλήν. ἐπειδὴ δὲ ἀπειρήκει, κατακλινόμενος 23
εἶπε, Τεκμήριον, ὦ ἄνδρες, ὅτι καλῶς γυμνά-
ζει καὶ τὰ ἐμὰ ὀρχήματα. ἐγὼ γοῦν διψῶ·
καὶ ὁ παῖς ἐγχεάτω μοι τὴν μεγάλην φιάλην.
Νὴ Δί᾽, ἔφη ὁ Καλλίας, καὶ ἡμῖν γε, ἐπεὶ
καὶ ἡμεῖς διψῶμεν ἐπὶ σοὶ γελῶντες. ὁ δ᾽ 24
αὖ Σωκράτης εἶπεν, Ἀλλὰ πίνειν μέν, ὦ ἄνδρες, καὶ ἐμοὶ πάνυ δοκεῖ· τῷ γὰρ ὄντι ὁ
οἶνος ἄρδων τὰς ψυχὰς τὰς μὲν λύπας ὥσπερ
ὁ μανδραγόρας τοὺς ἀνθρώπους κοιμίζει, τὰς
δὲ φιλοφροσύνας ὥσπερ ἔλαιον φλόγα ἐγείρει.
δοκεῖ μέντοι μοι καὶ τὰ τῶν ἀνδρῶν σώματα 25
ταὐτὰ πάσχειν ἅπερ καὶ τὰ τῶν ἐν γῇ φυο-
μένων. καὶ γὰρ ἐκεῖνα, ὅταν μὲν ὁ θεὸς αὐτὰ
ἄγαν ἀθρόως ποτίζῃ, οὐ δύναται ὀρθοῦσθαι
οὐδὲ ταῖς αὔραις διαπνεῖσθαι· ὅταν δ᾽ ὅσῳ
ἥδεται τοσοῦτο πίνῃ, καὶ μάλα ὀρθά τε

αὔξεται καὶ θάλλοντα ἀφικνεῖται εἰς τὴν καρ-
26 πογονίαν. οὕτω δὲ καὶ ἡμεῖς ἢν μὲν ἀθρόον
τὸ ποτὸν ἐγχεώμεθα, ταχὺ ἡμῖν καὶ τὰ σώματα καὶ αἱ γνῶμαι σφαλοῦνται, καὶ οὐδὲ
ἀναπνεῖν, μὴ ὅτι λέγειν τι δυνησόμεθα· ἢν
δὲ ἡμῖν οἱ παῖδες μικραῖς κύλιξι πυκνὰ ἐπι-
ψακάζωσιν, ἵνα καὶ ἐγὼ ἐν Γοργιείοις ῥήμα-
σιν εἴπω, οὕτως οὐ βιαζόμενοι ὑπὸ τοῦ οἴνου
μεθύειν ἀλλ᾽ ἀναπειθόμενοι πρὸς τὸ παιγνιω-
27 δέστερον ἀφιξόμεθα. ἐδόκει μὲν δὴ ταῦτα
πᾶσι· προσέθηκε δὲ ὁ Φίλιππος ὡς χρὴ τοὺς
οἰνοχόους μιμεῖσθαι τοὺς ἀγαθοὺς ἁρματηλά-
τας, θᾶττον περιελαύνοντας τὰς κύλικας. οἱ
μὲν δὴ οἰνοχόοι οὕτως ἐποίουν.

———◆———

CHAPTER III.

More music. Proposition to discuss something for mutual
pleasure and profit.

1   Ἐκ δὲ τούτου συνηρμοσμένῃ τῇ λύρᾳ πρὸς
τὸν αὐλὸν ἐκιθάρισεν ὁ παῖς καὶ ᾖσεν. ἔνθα
δὴ ἐπῄνεσαν μὲν ἅπαντες· ὁ δὲ Χαρμίδης
καὶ εἶπεν, Ἀλλ᾽ ἐμοὶ μὲν δοκεῖ, ὦ ἄνδρες,
ὥσπερ Σωκράτης ἔφη τὸν οἶνον, οὕτω καὶ
αὕτη ἡ κρᾶσις τῶν τε παίδων τῆς ὥρας καὶ
τῶν φθόγγων τὰς μὲν λύπας κοιμίζειν, τὴν δ᾽

ἀφροδίτην ἐγείρειν. ἐκ τούτου δὲ πάλιν εἶπεν 2
ὁ Σωκράτης, Οὗτοι μὲν δή, ὦ ἄνδρες, ἱκανοὶ
τέρπειν ἡμᾶς φαίνονται · ἡμεῖς δὲ τούτων
οἶδ' ὅτι πολὺ βελτίονες οἰόμεθα εἶναι · οὐκ
αἰσχρὸν οὖν εἰ μήδ' ἐπιχειρήσομεν συνόντες
ὠφελεῖν τι ἢ εὐφραίνειν ἀλλήλους ; ἐντεῦθεν
εἶπον πολλοί, Σὺ τοίνυν ἡμῖν ἐξηγοῦ ποίων
λόγων ἁπτόμενοι μάλιστ' ἂν ταῦτα ποιοῖμεν.
'Εγὼ μὲν τοίνυν, ἔφη, ἥδιστ' ἂν ἀπολάβοιμι 3
παρὰ Καλλίου τὴν ὑπόσχεσιν. ἔφη γὰρ δήπου, εἰ συνδειπνοῖμεν, ἐπιδείξειν τὴν αὑτοῦ
σοφίαν. Καὶ ἐπιδείξω γε, ἔφη, ἐὰν καὶ ὑμεῖς
ἅπαντες εἰς μέσον φέρητε ὅ τι ἕκαστος ἐπί-
στασθε ἀγαθόν. 'Αλλ' οὐδείς σοι, ἔφη, ἀντι-
λέγει τὸ μὴ οὐ λέξειν ὅ τι ἕκαστος ἡγεῖται
πλείστου ἄξιον ἐπίστασθαι.

By agreement each guest declares on what accomplishment
or possession he most prides himself.

'Εγὼ μὲν τοίνυν, ἔφη, λέγω ὑμῖν ἐφ' ᾧ 4
μέγιστον φρονῶ. ἀνθρώπους γὰρ οἶμαι ἱκανὸς
εἶναι βελτίους ποιεῖν. καὶ ὁ 'Αντισθένης εἶπε,
Πότερον τέχνην τινὰ βαναυσικὴν ἢ καλοκά-
γαθίαν διδάσκων ; Εἰ καλοκαγαθία ἐστὶν ἡ
δικαιοσύνη. Νὴ Δί', ἔφη ὁ 'Αντισθένης, ἥ
γε ἀναμφιλογωτάτη · ἐπείτοι ἀνδρεία μὲν καὶ
σοφία ἔστιν ὅτε βλαβερὰ καὶ φίλοις καὶ πόλει
δοκεῖ εἶναι, ἡ δὲ δικαιοσύνη οὐδὲ καθ' ἓν συμ-

5 μίγνυται τῇ ἀδικίᾳ. Ἐπειδὰν τοίνυν καὶ ἡμῶν
ἕκαστος εἴπῃ ὅ τι ὠφέλιμον ἔχει, τότε κἀγὼ
οὐ φθονήσω εἰπεῖν τὴν τέχνην δι' ἧς τοῦτο
ἀπεργάζομαι. ἀλλὰ σὺ αὖ, ἔφη, λέγε, ὦ Νι-
κήρατε, ἐπὶ ποίᾳ ἐπιστήμῃ μέγα φρονεῖς. καὶ
ὃς εἶπεν, Ὁ πατὴρ ἐπιμελούμενος ὅπως ἀνὴρ
ἀγαθὸς γενοίμην, ἠνάγκασέ με πάντα τὰ Ὁμή-
ρου ἔπη μαθεῖν· καὶ νῦν δυναίμην ἂν Ἰλιάδα
ὅλην καὶ Ὀδύσσειαν ἀπὸ στόματος εἰπεῖν.
6 Ἐκεῖνο δ', ἔφη ὁ Ἀντισθένης, λέληθέ σε ὅτι
καὶ οἱ ῥαψῳδοὶ πάντες ἐπίστανται ταῦτα τὰ
ἔπη; Καὶ πῶς ἄν, ἔφη, λελήθοι ἀκροώμενόν
γε αὐτῶν ὀλίγου ἀν' ἑκάστην ἡμέραν; Οἶσθά
τι οὖν ἔθνος, ἔφη, ἠλιθιώτερον ῥαψῳδῶν; Οὐ
μὰ τὸν Δί', ἔφη ὁ Νικήρατος, οὔκουν ἔμοιγε
δοκεῖ. Δῆλον γάρ, ἔφη ὁ Σωκράτης, ὅτι τὰς
ὑπονοίας οὐκ ἐπίστανται. σὺ δὲ Στησιμβρότῳ τε καὶ Ἀναξιμάνδρῳ καὶ ἄλλοις πολλοῖς πολὺ δέδωκας ἀργύριον, ὥστε οὐδέν σε
7 τῶν πολλοῦ ἀξίων λέληθε. τί γὰρ σύ, ἔφη,
ὦ Κριτόβουλε, ἐπὶ τίνι μέγιστον φρονεῖς;
Ἐπὶ κάλλει, ἔφη. Ἡ οὖν καὶ σύ, ἔφη ὁ
Σωκράτης, ἕξεις λέγειν ὅτι τῷ σῷ κάλλει
ἱκανὸς εἶ βελτίους ἡμᾶς ποιεῖν; Εἰ δὲ μή,
8 δῆλόν γε ὅτι φαῦλος φανοῦμαι. Τί γὰρ σύ,
εἶπεν, ἐπὶ τίνι μέγα φρονεῖς, ὦ Ἀντίσθενες;
Ἐπὶ πλούτῳ, ἔφη. ὁ μὲν δὴ Ἑρμογένης
ἀνήρετο εἰ πολὺ εἴη αὐτῷ ἀργύριον. ὁ δὲ

ἀπώμοσε μηδὲ ὀβολόν. Ἀλλὰ γῆν πολλὴν
κέκτησαι; Ἴσως ἄν, ἔφη, Αὐτολύκῳ τούτῳ
ἱκανὴ γένοιτο ἐγκονίσασθαι. Ἀκουστέον ἂν 9
εἴη καὶ σοῦ. τί γὰρ σύ, ἔφη, ὦ Χαρμίδη, ἐπὶ
τίνι μέγα φρονεῖς; Ἐγὼ αὖ, ἔφη, ἐπὶ πενίᾳ
μέγα φρονῶ. Νὴ Δί᾽, ἔφη ὁ Σωκράτης, ἐπ᾽
εὐχαρίστῳ γε πράγματι· τοῦτο γὰρ δὴ
ἥκιστα μὲν ἐπίφθονον, ἥκιστα δὲ περιμάχη-
τον, καὶ ἀφύλακτον ὂν σώζεται καὶ ἀμελού-
μενον ἰσχυρότερον γίγνεται. Σὺ δὲ δή, ἔφη 10
ὁ Καλλίας, ἐπὶ τίνι μέγα φρονεῖς, ὦ Σώκρατες; καὶ ὃς μάλα σεμνῶς ἀνασπάσας τὸ πρόσ-
ωπον Ἐπὶ μαστροπείᾳ εἶπεν. ἐπεὶ δὲ ἐγέλασαν ἐπ᾽ αὐτῷ, Ὑμεῖς μὲν γελᾶτε, ἔφη, ἐγὼ
δὲ οἶδ᾽ ὅτι καὶ πάνυ ἂν πολλὰ χρήματα λαμβάνοιμι, εἰ βουλοίμην χρῆσθαι τῇ τέχνῃ.
Σύ γε μὴν δῆλον, ἔφη ὁ Λύκων πρὸς τὸν 11
Φίλιππον, ὅτι ἐπὶ τῷ γελωτοποιεῖν μέγα φρονεῖς. Δικαιότερόν γ᾽, ἔφη, οἶμαι ἢ Καλλιπ-
πίδης ὁ ὑποκριτής, ὃς ὑπερσεμνύνεται ὅτι δύναται πολλοὺς κλαίοντας καθίζειν. Οὐκοῦν καὶ 12
σύ, ἔφη ὁ Ἀντισθένης, λέξεις, ὦ Λύκων, ἐπὶ
τίνι μέγα φρονεῖς; καὶ ὃς ἔφη, Οὐ γὰρ ἅπαντες ἴστε, ἔφη, ὅτι ἐπὶ τούτῳ τῷ υἱεῖ; Οὗτός
γε μήν, ἔφη τις, δῆλον ὅτι ἐπὶ τῷ νικηφόρος
εἶναι. καὶ ὁ Αὐτόλυκος ἀνερυθριάσας εἶπε,
Μὰ Δί᾽ οὐκ ἔγωγε. ἐπεὶ δὲ ἅπαντες ἡσθέν- 13
τες ὅτι ἤκουσαν αὐτοῦ φωνήσαντος προσ-

ἔβλεψαν, ἤρετό τις αὐτόν, Ἀλλ᾿ ἐπὶ τῷ μήν,
ὦ Αὐτόλυκε ; ὁ δ᾿ εἶπεν, Ἐπὶ τῷ πατρί, καὶ
ἅμα ἐνεκλίθη αὐτῷ. καὶ ὁ Καλλίας ἰδών,
Ἆρ᾿ οἶσθα, ἔφη, ὦ Λύκων, ὅτι πλουσιώτατος
εἶ ἀνθρώπων ; Μὰ Δί᾿, ἔφη, τοῦτο μέντοι
ἐγὼ οὐκ οἶδα. Ἀλλὰ λανθάνει σε ὅτι οὐκ
ἂν δέξαιο τὰ βασιλέως χρήματα ἀντὶ τοῦ
υἱοῦ ; Ἐπ᾿ αὐτοφώρῳ εἴλημμαι, ἔφη, πλου-
14 σιώτατος, ὡς ἔοικεν, ἀνθρώπων ὤν. Σὺ δέ,
ἔφη ὁ Νικήρατος, ὦ Ἑρμόγενες, ἐπὶ τίνι μάλιστα ἀγάλλει ; καὶ ὅς, Ἐπὶ φίλων, ἔφη,
ἀρετῇ καὶ δυνάμει, καὶ ὅτι τοιοῦτοι ὄντες
ἐμοῦ ἐπιμέλονται. ἐνταῦθα τοίνυν πάντες
προσέβλεψαν αὐτῷ, καὶ πολλοὶ ἅμα ἤροντο
εἰ καὶ σφίσι δηλώσει αὐτούς. ὁ δὲ εἶπεν ὅτι
οὐ φθονήσει.

CHAPTER IV.

Consideration of the several claims, or boasts. Callias—
would improve men's morals.

1 Ἐκ τούτου ἔλεξεν ὁ Σωκράτης, Οὐκοῦν λοι-
πὸν ἂν εἴη ἡμῖν ἃ ἕκαστος ὑπέσχετο ἀποδεικνύναι ὡς πολλοῦ ἄξιά ἐστιν. Ἀκούοιτ᾿ ἄν,
ἔφη ὁ Καλλίας, ἐμοῦ πρῶτον. ἐγὼ γὰρ ἐν
τῷ χρόνῳ ᾧ ὑμῶν ἀκούω ἀπορούντων τί τὸ
δίκαιον, ἐν τούτῳ δικαιοτέρους τοὺς ἀνθρώπους ποιῶ. καὶ ὁ Σωκράτης, Πῶς, ὦ λῷστε ;

ἔφη. Διδοὺς νὴ Δί' ἀργύριον. καὶ ὁ 'Αντι- 2
σθένης ἐπαναστὰς μάλα ἐλεγκτικῶς αὐτὸν
ἐπήρετο, Οἱ δὲ ἄνθρωποι, ὦ Καλλία, πότερον
ἐν ταῖς ψυχαῖς ἢ ἐν τῷ βαλαντίῳ τὸ δίκαιόν
σοι δοκοῦσιν ἔχειν; 'Εν ταῖς ψυχαῖς, ἔφη.
Κᾆπειτα σὺ εἰς τὸ βαλάντιον διδοὺς ἀργύριον
τὰς ψυχὰς δικαιοτέρας ποιεῖς; Μάλιστα.
Πῶς; "Οτι διὰ τὸ εἰδέναι ὡς ἔστιν ὅτου
πριάμενοι τὰ ἐπιτήδεια ἕξουσιν οὐκ ἐθέλουσι
κακουργοῦντες κινδυνεύειν. Ἦ καί σοι, ἔφη, 3
ἀποδιδόασιν ὅ τι ἂν λάβωσι; Μὰ τὸν Δί',
ἔφη, οὐ μὲν δή. Τί δέ, ἀντὶ τοῦ ἀργυρίου
χάριτας; Οὐ μὰ τὸν Δί', ἔφη, οὐδὲ τοῦτο,
ἀλλ' ἔνιοι καὶ ἐχθιόνως ἔχουσιν ἢ πρὶν λα-
βεῖν. Θαυμαστά γ', ἔφη ὁ 'Αντισθένης ἅμα
εἰσβλέπων ὡς ἐλέγχων αὐτόν, εἰ πρὸς μὲν
τοὺς ἄλλους δύνασαι δικαίους ποιεῖν αὐτούς,
πρὸς δὲ σαυτὸν οὔ. Καὶ τί τοῦτ', ἔφη ὁ 4
Καλλίας, θαυμαστόν; οὐ καὶ τέκτονάς τε καὶ
οἰκοδόμους πολλοὺς ὁρᾷς οἳ ἄλλοις μὲν πολλοῖς ποιοῦσιν οἰκίας, ἑαυτοῖς δὲ οὐ δύνανται
ποιῆσαι, ἀλλ' ἐν μισθωταῖς οἰκοῦσι; καὶ
ἀνάσχου μέντοι, ὦ σοφιστά, ἐλεγχόμενος.
Νὴ Δί', ἔφη ὁ Σωκράτης, ἀνεχέσθω μέντοι · 5
ἐπεὶ καὶ οἱ μάντεις λέγονται δήπου ἄλλοις
μὲν προαγορεύειν τὸ μέλλον, ἑαυτοῖς δὲ μὴ
προορᾶν τὸ ἐπιόν. οὗτος μὲν δὴ ὁ λόγος
ἐνταῦθα ἔληξεν.

Niceratus : his knowledge of the ancient epics.

6 Ἐκ τούτου δὲ ὁ Νικήρατος, Ἀκούοιτ' ἂν, ἔφη, καὶ ἐμοῦ ἃ ἔσεσθε βελτίονες, ἢν ἐμοὶ συνῆτε. ἴστε γὰρ δήπου ὅτι Ὅμηρος ὁ σοφώτατος πεποίηκε σχεδὸν περὶ πάντων τῶν ἀνθρωπίνων. ὅστις ἂν οὖν ὑμῶν βούληται ἢ οἰκονομικὸς ἢ δημηγορικὸς ἢ στρατηγικὸς γενέσθαι ἢ ὅμοιος Ἀχιλλεῖ ἢ Αἴαντι ἢ Νέστορι ἢ Ὀδυσσεῖ, ἐμὲ θεραπευέτω. ἐγὼ γὰρ ταῦτα πάντα ἐπίσταμαι. Ἦ καὶ βασιλεύειν, ἔφη ὁ Ἀντισθένης, ἐπίστασαι, ὅτι οἶσθα ἐπαινέσαντα αὐτὸν τὸν Ἀγαμέμνονα ὡς βασιλεύς τε εἴη ἀγαθὸς κρατερός τ' αἰχμητής; Καὶ ναὶ μὰ Δί', ἔφη, ἔγωγε ὅτι ἁρματηλατοῦντα δεῖ ἐγγὺς μὲν τῆς στήλης κάμψαι·

αὐτὸν δὲ κλινθῆναι ἐυξέστου ἐπὶ δίφρου
ἧκ' ἐπ' ἀριστερὰ τοῖν, ἀτὰρ τὸν δεξιὸν ἵππον
κένσαι ὁμοκλήσαντ' εἶξαί τέ οἱ ἡνία χερσί.

7 καὶ πρὸς τούτοις γε ἄλλο οἶδα, καὶ ὑμῖν αὐτίκα μάλ' ἔξεστι πειρᾶσθαι. εἶπε γάρ που Ὅμηρος Ἐπὶ δὲ κρόμυον, ποτῷ ὄψον. ἐὰν οὖν ἐνέγκῃ τις κρόμμυον, αὐτίκα μάλα τοῦτό γε ὠφελημένοι ἔσεσθε· ἥδιον γὰρ πιεῖ-
8 σθε. καὶ ὁ Χαρμίδης εἶπεν, Ὦ ἄνδρες, ὁ Νικήρατος κρομμύων ὄζων ἐπιθυμεῖ οἴκαδε ἐλθεῖν, ἵν' ἡ γυνὴ αὐτοῦ πιστεύῃ μὴ διανοη-

θῆναι μηδένα ἂν φιλῆσαι αὐτόν. Νὴ Δί',
ἔφη ὁ Σωκράτης, ἀλλ' ἄλλην που δόξαν
γελοίαν κίνδυνος ἡμῖν προσλαβεῖν. ὄψον
μὲν γὰρ δὴ ὄντως ἔοικεν εἶναι, ὡς κρόμμυόν γε
οὐ μόνον σῖτον ἀλλὰ καὶ ποτὸν ἡδύνει. εἰ
δὲ δὴ τοῦτο καὶ μετὰ δεῖπνον τρωξόμεθα,
ὅπως μὴ φήσῃ τις ἡμᾶς πρὸς Καλλίαν ἐλθόν-
τας ἡδυπαθεῖν. Μηδαμῶς, ἔφη, ὦ Σώκρατες. 9
εἰς μὲν γὰρ μάχην ὁρμωμένῳ καλῶς ἔχει
κρόμμυον ὑποτρώγειν, ὥσπερ ἔνιοι τοὺς ἀλεκ-
τρυόνας σκόροδα σιτίσαντες συμβάλλουσιν·
ἡμεῖς δὲ ἴσως βουλευόμεθα ὅπως φιλήσομέν
τινα μᾶλλον ἢ μαχούμεθα. καὶ οὗτος μὲν
δὴ ὁ λόγος οὕτω πως ἐπαύσατο.

Critobulus: his personal beauty.

Ὁ δὲ Κριτόβουλος, Οὐκοῦν αὖ ἐγὼ λέξω, 10
ἔφη, ἐξ ὧν ἐπὶ τῷ κάλλει μέγα φρονῶ.
Λέγε, ἔφασαν. Εἰ μὲν τοίνυν μὴ καλός εἰμί,
ὡς οἶμαι, ὑμεῖς ἂν δικαίως ἀπάτης δίκην
ὑπέχοιτε· οὐδενὸς γὰρ ὁρκίζοντος ἀεὶ ὀμνύ-
οντες καλόν μέ φατε εἶναι. κἀγὼ μέντοι
πιστεύω. καλοὺς γὰρ καὶ ἀγαθοὺς ὑμᾶς
ἄνδρας νομίζω. εἰ δ' εἰμί τε τῷ ὄντι καλὸς 11
καὶ ὑμεῖς τὰ αὐτὰ πρὸς ἐμὲ πάσχετε οἷάπερ
ἐγὼ πρὸς τὸν ἐμοὶ δοκοῦντα καλὸν εἶναι,
ὄμνυμι πάντας θεοὺς μὴ ἑλέσθαι ἂν τὴν βασιλέως ἀρχὴν ἀντὶ τοῦ καλὸς εἶναι. νῦν γὰρ 12

ἐγὼ **Κλεινίαν** ἥδιον μὲν θεῶμαι ἢ τἆλλα
πάντα τὰ ἐν ἀνθρώποις καλά · τυφλὸς δὲ
τῶν ἄλλων ἁπάντων μᾶλλον δεξαίμην ἂν
εἶναι ἢ ἐκείνου καὶ ἑνὸς ὄντος · ἄχθομαι
δὲ καὶ νυκτὶ καὶ ὕπνῳ, ὅτι ἐκεῖνον οὐχ
ὁρῶ, ἡμέρᾳ δὲ καὶ ἡλίῳ τὴν μεγίστην χάριν
13 οἶδα, ὅτι μοι **Κλεινίαν** ἀναφαίνουσιν. ἄξιόν
γε μὴν ἡμῖν τοῖς καλοῖς καὶ ἐπὶ τοῖσδε μέγα
φρονεῖν, ὅτι τὸν μὲν ἰσχυρὸν πονοῦντα δεῖ
κτᾶσθαι τἀγαθὰ καὶ τὸν ἀνδρεῖον κινδυνεύ-
οντα, τὸν δέ γε σοφὸν λέγοντα · ὁ δὲ καλὸς
καὶ ἡσυχίαν ἔχων πάντ᾽ ἂν διαπράξαιτο.
14 ἐγὼ γοῦν, καίπερ εἰδὼς ὅτι χρήματα ἡδὺ κτῆμα, ἥδιον μὲν ἂν **Κλεινίᾳ** τὰ ὄντα διδοίην ἢ
ἕτερα παρ᾽ ἄλλου λαμβάνοιμι, ἥδιον δ᾽ ἂν
δουλεύοιμι ἢ ἐλεύθερος εἴην, εἴ μου **Κλεινίας**
ἄρχειν ἐθέλοι. καὶ γὰρ πονοίην ἂν ῥᾷον
ἐκείνῳ ἢ ἀναπαυοίμην, καὶ κινδυνεύοιμ᾽ ἂν
15 πρὸ ἐκείνου ἥδιον ἢ ἀκίνδυνος ζῴην. ὥστε εἰ
σύ, ὦ **Καλλία**, μέγα φρονεῖς ὅτι δικαιοτέρους
δύνασαι ποιεῖν, ἐγὼ πρὸς πᾶσαν ἀρετὴν δι-
καιότερος σοῦ εἰμι ἄγειν ἀνθρώπους. διὰ γὰρ
τὸ ἐμπνεῖν τι ἡμᾶς τοὺς καλοὺς τοῖς ἐρωτι-
κοῖς ἐλευθεριωτέρους μὲν αὐτοὺς ποιοῦμεν
εἰς χρήματα, φιλοπονωτέρους δὲ καὶ φιλοκα-
λωτέρους ἐν τοῖς κινδύνοις, καὶ μὴν αἰδημο-
16 νεστέρους τε καὶ ἐγκρατεστέρους. μαίνον-
ται δὲ καὶ οἱ μὴ τοὺς καλοὺς στρατηγοὺς

αἱρούμενοι. ἐγὼ γοῦν μετὰ Κλεινίου κἂν διὰ
πυρὸς ἰοίην· οἶδα δ᾽ ὅτι καὶ ὑμεῖς μετ᾽ ἐμοῦ.
ὥστε μηκέτι ἀπόρει, ὦ Σώκρατες, εἴ τι τοὐ-
μὸν κάλλος ἀνθρώπους ὠφελήσει. ἀλλ᾽ οὐδὲ 17
μέντοι ταύτῃ γε ἀτιμαστέον τὸ κάλλος ὡς
ταχὺ παρακμάζον, ἐπεὶ ὥσπερ γε παῖς γίγνεται καλός, οὕτω καὶ μειράκιον καὶ ἀνὴρ
καὶ πρεσβύτης. τεκμήριον δέ· θαλλοφόρους
γὰρ τῇ Ἀθηνᾷ τοὺς καλοὺς γέροντας ἐκλέγον-
ται, ὡς συμπαρομαρτοῦντος πάσῃ ἡλικίᾳ τοῦ
κάλλους. εἰ δὲ ἡδὺ τὸ παρ᾽ ἑκόντων δια- 18
πράττεσθαι ὧν τις δέοιτο, εὖ οἶδ᾽ ὅτι καὶ νυνὶ
θᾶττον ἂν ἐγὼ καὶ σιωπῶν πείσαιμι τὸν παῖδα
τόνδε καὶ τὴν παῖδα φιλῆσαί με ἢ σύ, ὦ
Σώκρατες, εἰ καὶ πάνυ πολλὰ καὶ σοφὰ λέ-
γοις. Τί τοῦτο; ἔφη ὁ Σωκράτης· ὡς γὰρ 19
καὶ ἐμοῦ καλλίων ὢν ταῦτα κομπάζεις; Νὴ
Δί᾽, ἔφη ὁ Κριτόβουλος, ἢ πάντων Σειληνῶν
τῶν ἐν τοῖς σατυρικοῖς αἴσχιστος ἂν εἴην.
[ὁ δὲ Σωκράτης καὶ ἐτύγχανε προσεμφερὴς
τούτοις ὤν.] Ἄγε νυν, ἔφη ὁ Σωκράτης, 20
ὅπως μεμνήσει διακριθῆναι περὶ τοῦ κάλλους,
ἐπειδὰν οἱ προκείμενοι λόγοι περιέλθωσι· κρι-
νάτω δ᾽ ἡμᾶς μὴ Ἀλέξανδρος ὁ Πριάμου,
ἀλλ᾽ αὐτοὶ οὗτοι οὕσπερ σὺ οἴει ἐπιθυμεῖν σε
φιλῆσαι.

[*Critobulus amid the banter of the company continues
still further his silly raving over his friend Cleinias.*]

Charmides : his poverty a blessing.

29 Ὁ δὲ Καλλίας, Σὸν μέρος, ἔφη, λέγειν, ὦ
Χαρμίδη, διότι ἐπὶ πενίᾳ μέγα φρονεῖς. Οὐκοῦν τόδε μέν, ἔφη, ὁμολογεῖται, κρεῖττον εἶναι
θαρρεῖν ἢ φοβεῖσθαι καὶ ἐλεύθερον εἶναι μᾶλλον ἢ δουλεύειν καὶ θεραπεύεσθαι μᾶλλον ἢ
θεραπεύειν καὶ πιστεύεσθαι ὑπὸ τῆς πατρί-
30 δος μᾶλλον ἢ ἀπιστεῖσθαι. ἐγὼ τοίνυν ἐν
τῇδε τῇ πόλει ὅτε μὲν πλούσιος ἦν πρῶτον
μὲν ἐφοβούμην μή τίς μου τὴν οἰκίαν διορύ-
ξας καὶ τὰ χρήματα λάβοι καὶ αὐτόν τί με
κακὸν ἐργάσαιτο· ἔπειτα δὲ καὶ τοὺς συκο-
φάντας ἐθεράπευον, εἰδὼς ὅτι παθεῖν μᾶλλον
κακῶς ἱκανὸς εἴην ἢ ποιῆσαι ἐκείνους. καὶ
γὰρ δὴ καὶ προσετάττετο μὲν ἀεί τί μοι
δαπανᾶν ὑπὸ τῆς πόλεως, ἀποδημῆσαι δὲ οὐ-
31 δαμοῦ ἐξῆν. νῦν δ' ἐπειδὴ τῶν ὑπερορίων
στέρομαι καὶ τὰ ἔγγαια οὐ καρποῦμαι καὶ
τὰ ἐκ τῆς οἰκίας πέπραται, ἡδέως μὲν κα-
θεύδω ἐκτεταμένος, πιστὸς δὲ τῇ πόλει γεγένημαι, οὐκέτι δὲ ἀπειλοῦμαι, ἀλλ' ἤδη ἀπειλῶ
ἄλλοις, ὡς ἐλευθέρῳ τε ἔξεστί μοι καὶ ἀπο-
δημεῖν καὶ ἐπιδημεῖν· ὑπανίστανται δέ μοι
ἤδη καὶ θάκων καὶ ὁδῶν ἐξίστανται οἱ πλού-
32 σιοι. καὶ εἰμὶ νῦν μὲν τυράννῳ ἐοικώς, τότε
δὲ σαφῶς δοῦλος ἦν· καὶ τότε μὲν ἐγὼ φόρον ἀπέφερον τῷ δήμῳ, νῦν δὲ ἡ πόλις τέλος

φέρουσα τρέφει με. ἀλλὰ καὶ Σωκράτει, ὅτε
μὲν πλούσιος ἦν, ἐλοιδόρουν με ὅτι συνῆν,
νῦν δ᾽ ἐπεὶ πένης γεγένημαι, οὐκέτι οὐδὲν
μέλει οὐδενί. καὶ μὴν ὅτε μέν γε πολλὰ
εἶχον, ἀεί τι ἀπέβαλλον ἢ ὑπὸ τῆς πόλεως
ἢ ὑπὸ τῆς τύχης· νῦν δὲ ἀποβάλλω μὲν
οὐδέν, οὐδὲ γὰρ ἔχω, ἀεὶ δέ τι λήψεσθαι
ἐλπίζω. Οὐκοῦν, ἔφη ὁ Καλλίας, καὶ εὔχει 33
μηδέποτε πλουτεῖν, καὶ ἐάν τι ὄναρ ἀγαθὸν
ἴδῃς, τοῖς ἀποτροπαίοις θύεις ; Μὰ Δία τοῦτο
μέντοι, ἔφη, ἐγὼ οὐ ποιῶ, ἀλλὰ μάλα φιλο-
κινδύνως ὑπομένω, ἤν ποθέν τι ἐλπίζω λήψεσθαι.

Antisthenes : his wealth (not of purse).

᾽Αλλ᾽ ἄγε δή, ἔφη ὁ Σωκράτης, σὺ αὖ 34
λέγε ἡμῖν, ὦ ᾽Αντίσθενες, πῶς οὕτω βραχέα
ἔχων μέγα φρονεῖς ἐπὶ πλούτῳ. Ὅτι νομίζω, ὦ ἄνδρες, τοὺς ἀνθρώπους οὐκ ἐν τῷ
οἴκῳ τὸν πλοῦτον καὶ τὴν πενίαν ἔχειν ἀλλ᾽
ἐν ταῖς ψυχαῖς. ὁρῶ γὰρ πολλοὺς μὲν ἰδιώ- 35
τας, οἳ πάνυ πολλὰ ἔχοντες χρήματα οὕτω
πένεσθαι ἡγοῦνται ὥστε πάντα μὲν πόνον,
πάντα δὲ κίνδυνον ὑποδύονται, ἐφ᾽ ᾧ πλείονα
κτήσονται, οἶδα δὲ καὶ ἀδελφούς, οἳ τὰ ἴσα
λαχόντες ὁ μὲν αὐτῶν τἀρκοῦντα ἔχει καὶ
περιττεύοντα τῆς δαπάνης, ὁ δὲ τοῦ παντὸς
ἐνδεῖται· αἰσθάνομαι δὲ καὶ τυράννους τινάς, 36

οἳ οὕτω πεινῶσι χρημάτων ὥστε ποιοῦσι
πολὺ δεινότερα τῶν ἀπορωτάτων· δι᾽ ἔνδειαν
μὲν γὰρ δήπου οἱ μὲν κλέπτουσιν, οἱ δὲ τοι-
χωρυχοῦσιν, οἱ δὲ ἀνδραποδίζονται· τύραννοι
δ᾽ εἰσί τινες οἳ ὅλους μὲν οἴκους ἀναιροῦσιν,
ἀθρόους δ᾽ ἀποκτείνουσι, πολλάκις δὲ καὶ
ὅλας πόλεις χρημάτων ἕνεκα ἐξανδραποδί-
37 ζονται.   τούτους μὲν οὖν ἔγωγε καὶ πάνυ
οἰκτείρω τῆς ἄγαν χαλεπῆς νόσου.   ὅμοια γάρ
μοι δοκοῦσι πάσχειν ὥσπερ εἴ τις [πολλὰ
ἔχων καὶ] πολλὰ ἐσθίων μηδέποτε ἐμπί-
πλαιτο.   ἐγὼ δὲ οὕτω μὲν πολλὰ ἔχω ὡς
μόλις αὐτὰ καὶ ἐγὼ αὐτὸς εὑρίσκω· ὅμως
δὲ περίεστί μοι καὶ ἐσθίοντι ἄχρι τοῦ μὴ
πεινῆν ἀφικέσθαι καὶ πίνοντι μέχρι τοῦ μὴ
διψῆν καὶ ἀμφιέννυσθαι ὥστε ἔξω μὲν μηδὲν
μᾶλλον Καλλίου τούτου τοῦ πλουσιωτάτου
38 ῥιγῶν·   ἐπειδάν γε μὴν ἐν τῇ οἰκίᾳ γένωμαι,
πάνυ μὲν ἀλεεινοὶ χιτῶνες οἱ τοῖχοί μοι δοκοῦσιν εἶναι, πάνυ δὲ παχεῖαι ἐφεστρίδες οἱ ὄροφοι,
στρωμνήν γε μὴν οὕτως ἀρκοῦσαν ἔχω ὥστ᾽
39 ἔργον μέ γ᾽ ἐστὶ καὶ ἀνεγεῖραι.   καὶ πάντα
τοίνυν ταῦτα οὕτως ἡδέα μοι δοκεῖ εἶναι ὡς
μᾶλλον μὲν ἥδεσθαι ποιῶν ἕκαστα αὐτῶν οὐκ
ἂν εὐξαίμην, ἧττον δέ· οὕτω μοι δοκεῖ ἔνια
40 αὐτῶν ἡδίω εἶναι τοῦ συμφέροντος.   πλείστου
δ᾽ ἄξιον κτῆμα ἐν τῷ ἐμῷ πλούτῳ λογίζομαι
εἶναι ἐκεῖνο ὅτι εἴ μού τις καὶ τὰ νῦν ὄντα

παρέλοιτο, οὐδὲν οὕτως ὁρῶ φαῦλον ἔργον
ὁποῖον οὐκ ἀρκοῦσαν ἂν τροφὴν ἐμοὶ παρέχοι.
καὶ γὰρ ὅταν ἡδυπαθῆσαι βουληθῶ, οὐκ ἐκ 41
τῆς ἀγορᾶς τὰ τίμια ὠνοῦμαι, πολυτελῆ γὰρ
γίγνεται, ἀλλ᾽ ἐκ τῆς ψυχῆς ταμιεύομαι. καὶ
πολὺ πλεῖον διαφέρει πρὸς ἡδονήν, ὅταν ἀνα-
μείνας τὸ δεηθῆναι προσφέρωμαι ἢ ὅταν τινὶ
τῶν τιμίων χρῶμαι, ὥσπερ καὶ νῦν τῷδε τῷ
Θασίῳ οἴνῳ ἐντυχὼν οὐ διψῶν πίνω αὐτόν.
ἀλλὰ μὴν καὶ πολὺ δικαιοτέρους γε εἰκὸς 42
εἶναι τοὺς εὐτέλειαν μᾶλλον ἢ πολυχρημα-
τίαν σκοποῦντας. οἷς γὰρ μάλιστα τὰ παρόντα ἀρκεῖ ἥκιστα τῶν ἀλλοτρίων ὀρέγονται.
ἄξιον δ᾽ ἐννοῆσαι ὡς καὶ ἐλευθερίους ὁ τοιοῦ- 43
τος πλοῦτος παρέχεται. ‖ Σωκράτης τε γὰρ
οὗτος παρ᾽ οὗ ἐγὼ τοῦτον ἐκτησάμην οὔτ᾽
ἀριθμῷ οὔτε σταθμῷ ἐπήρκει μοι, ἀλλ᾽ ὁπό-
σον ἐδυνάμην φέρεσθαι, τοσοῦτόν μοι παρε-
δίδου · ἐγώ τε νῦν οὐδενὶ φθονῶ, ἀλλὰ πᾶσι
τοῖς φίλοις καὶ ἐπιδεικνύω τὴν ἀφθονίαν καὶ
μεταδίδωμι τῷ βουλομένῳ τοῦ ἐν τῇ ἐμῇ
ψυχῇ πλούτου. καὶ μὴν καὶ τὸ ἁβρότατόν γε 44
κτῆμα τὴν σχολὴν ἀεὶ ὁρᾶτέ μοι παροῦσαν,
ὥστε καὶ θεᾶσθαι τὰ ἀξιοθέατα καὶ ἀκούειν
τὰ ἀξιάκουστα καὶ ὃ πλείστου ἐγὼ τιμῶμαι,
Σωκράτει σχολάζων συνδιημερεύειν. καὶ οὗτος
δὲ οὐ τοὺς πλεῖστον ἀριθμοῦντας χρυσίον θαυ-
μάζει, ἀλλ᾽ οἳ ἂν αὐτῷ ἀρέσκωσι τούτοις συνὼν

45 διατελεῖ. οὗτος μὲν οὖν οὕτως εἶπεν. ὁ δὲ
Καλλίας, Νὴ τὴν ῞Ηραν, ἔφη, τά τε ἄλλα
ζηλῶ σε τοῦ πλούτου καὶ ὅτι οὔτε ἡ πόλις
σοι ἐπιτάττουσα ὡς δούλῳ χρῆται οὔτε οἱ
ἄνθρωποι, ἢν μὴ δανείσῃς, ὀργίζονται. ᾽Αλλὰ
μὰ Δί᾽, ἔφη ὁ Νικήρατος, μὴ ζήλου· ἐγὼ
γὰρ ἥξω παρ᾽ αὐτοῦ δανεισόμενος τὸ μηδενὸς
προσδεῖσθαι· οὕτω πεπαιδευμένος ὑπὸ ῾Ομή-
ρου ἀριθμεῖν

     ἔπτ᾽ ἀπύρους τρίποδας, δέκα δὲ χρυσοῖο τάλαντα,
     αἴθωνας δὲ λέβητας ἐείκοσι, δώδεκα δ᾽ ἵππους,

σταθμῷ καὶ ἀριθμῷ ὡς πλείστου πλούτου
ἐπιθυμῶν οὐ παύομαι· ἐξ ὧν ἴσως καὶ φιλο-
χρηματώτερός τισι δοκῶ εἶναι. ἔνθα δὴ ἀνε-
γέλασαν ἅπαντες, νομίζοντες τὰ ὄντα εἰρη-
κέναι αὐτόν.

Hermogenes: his friends (the Gods).

46 ᾽Εκ τούτου εἶπέ τις, Σὸν ἔργον, ὦ ῾Ερμό-
γενες, λέγειν τε τοὺς φίλους οἵτινές εἰσι καὶ
ἐπιδεικνύναι ὡς μέγα τε δύνανται καὶ σοῦ
ἐπιμέλονται, ἵνα δοκῇς δικαίως ἐπ᾽ αὐτοῖς
47 μέγα φρονεῖν. Οὐκοῦν ὡς μὲν καὶ ῞Ελληνες
καὶ βάρβαροι τοὺς θεοὺς ἡγοῦνται πάντα
εἰδέναι τά τε ὄντα καὶ τὰ μέλλοντα εὔδηλον.
πᾶσαι γοῦν αἱ πόλεις καὶ πάντα τὰ ἔθνη
διὰ μαντικῆς ἐπερωτῶσι τοὺς θεοὺς τί τε
χρὴ καὶ τί οὐ χρὴ ποιεῖν. καὶ μὴν ὅτι νομί-

ζομέν γε δύνασθαι αὐτοὺς καὶ εὖ καὶ κακῶς
ποιεῖν καὶ τοῦτο σαφές. πάντες γοῦν αἰτοῦν-
ται τοὺς θεοὺς τὰ μὲν φαῦλα ἀποτρέπειν,
τἀγαθὰ δὲ διδόναι. οὗτοι τοίνυν οἱ πάντα 48
μὲν εἰδότες πάντα δὲ δυνάμενοι θεοὶ οὕτω
μοι φίλοι εἰσὶν ὥστε διὰ τὸ ἐπιμελεῖσθαί
μου οὔποτε λήθω αὐτοὺς οὔτε νυκτὸς οὔθ᾽
ἡμέρας οὔθ᾽ ὅποι ἂν ὁρμῶμαι οὔθ᾽ ὅ τι ἂν
μέλλω πράττειν. διὰ δὲ τὸ προειδέναι καὶ
ὅ τι ἐξ ἑκάστου ἀποβήσεται σημαίνουσί μοι
πέμποντες ἀγγέλους φήμας καὶ ἐνύπνια καὶ
οἰωνοὺς ἅ τε δεῖ καὶ ἃ οὐ χρὴ ποιεῖν, οἷς
ἐγὼ ὅταν μὲν πείθωμαι, οὐδέποτέ μοι μετα-
μέλει· ἤδη δέ ποτε καὶ ἀπιστήσας ἐκολά-
σθην. καὶ ὁ Σωκράτης εἶπεν, Ἀλλὰ τούτων 49
μὲν οὐδὲν ἄπιστον. ἐκεῖνο μέντοι ἔγωγε
ἡδέως ἂν πυθοίμην, πῶς αὐτοὺς θεραπεύων
οὕτω φίλους ἔχεις. Ναὶ μὰ τὸν Δί᾽, ἔφη ὁ
Ἑρμογένης, καὶ μάλα εὐτελῶς. ἐπαινῶ τε
γὰρ αὐτοὺς οὐδὲν δαπανῶν, ὧν τε διδόασιν
ἀεὶ αὖ παρέχομαι, εὐφημῶ τε ὅσα ἂν δύνωμαι καὶ ἐφ᾽ οἷς ἂν αὐτοὺς μάρτυρας ποιήσω-
μαι ἑκὼν οὐδὲν ψεύδομαι. Νὴ Δί᾽, ἔφη
ὁ Σωκράτης, εἰ ἄρα τοιοῦτος ὢν φίλους
αὐτοὺς ἔχεις, καὶ οἱ θεοί, ὡς ἔοικε, καλο-
κἀγαθίᾳ ἥδονται. οὗτος μὲν δὴ ὁ λόγος
οὕτως ἐσπουδαιολογήθη.

Philip : his buffoonery.   The Syracusan : simpletons.

50   Ἐπειδὴ δὲ εἰς τὸν Φίλιππον ἧκον, ἠρώ-
των αὐτὸν τί ὁρῶν ἐν τῇ γελωτοποιίᾳ μέγα
ἐπ᾽ αὐτῇ φρονοίη. Οὐ γὰρ ἄξιον, ἔφη, ὁπότε
γε πάντες εἰδότες ὅτι γελωτοποιός εἰμι, ὅταν
μέν τι ἀγαθὸν ἔχωσι, παρακαλοῦσί με ἐπὶ
ταῦτα προθύμως, ὅταν δὲ κακόν τι λάβωσι,
φεύγουσιν ἀμεταστρεπτί, φοβούμενοι μὴ καὶ
51 ἄκοντες γελάσωσι ; καὶ ὁ Νικήρατος εἶπε,
Νὴ Δία, σὺ τοίνυν δικαίως μέγα φρονεῖς.
ἐμοὶ γὰρ αὖ τῶν φίλων οἱ μὲν εὖ πράττον-
τες ἐκποδὼν ἀπέρχονται, οἳ δ᾽ ἂν κακόν τι
λάβωσι, γενεαλογοῦσι τὴν συγγένειαν καὶ οὐδέ-
52 ποτέ μου ἀπολείπονται. Εἶεν· σὺ δὲ δή,
ἔφη ὁ Χαρμίδης, ὦ Συρακόσιε, ἐπὶ τῷ μέγα
φρονεῖς ; ἢ δῆλον ὅτι ἐπὶ τῷ παιδί ; Μὰ
τὸν Δί᾽, ἔφη, οὐ μὲν δή· ἀλλὰ καὶ δέδοικα
περὶ αὐτοῦ ἰσχυρῶς. αἰσθάνομαι γάρ τινας
55 ἐπιβουλεύοντας διαφθεῖραι αὐτόν. Ἀλλ᾽ ἐπὶ
τῷ μήν ; Ἐπὶ νὴ Δία τοῖς ἄφροσιν. οὗτοι
γὰρ τὰ ἐμὰ νευρόσπαστα θεώμενοι τρέφουσί
με. Ταῦτα γάρ, ἔφη ὁ Φίλιππος, καὶ πρώην
ἐγώ σου ἤκουον εὐχομένου πρὸς τοὺς θεοὺς
ὅπου ἂν ᾖς διδόναι καρποῦ μὲν ἀφθονίαν,
φρενῶν δὲ ἀφορίαν.

Socrates : his abilities as a go-between.

Εἶεν, ἔφη ὁ Καλλίας· σὺ δὲ δή, ὦ 56
Σώκρατες, τί ἔχεις εἰπεῖν ὡς ἄξιόν σοί ἐστι
μέγα φρονεῖν ἐφ᾽ ᾗ εἶπας οὕτως ἀδόξῳ οὔσῃ
τέχνῃ ; καὶ ὃς εἶπεν, Ὁμολογησώμεθα πρῶτον ποῖά ἐστιν ἔργα τοῦ μαστροποῦ· καὶ
ὅσα ἂν ἐρωτῶ, μὴ ὀκνεῖτε ἀποκρίνεσθαι, ἵνα
εἰδῶμεν ὅσα ἂν συνομολογῶμεν. καὶ ὑμῖν
οὕτω δοκεῖ ; ἔφη. Πάνυ μὲν οὖν, ἔφασαν.
ὡς δ᾽ ἅπαξ εἶπον Πάνυ μὲν οὖν, τοῦτο
πάντες ἐκ τοῦ λοιποῦ ἀπεκρίναντο. Οὐκοῦν 57
ἀγαθοῦ μέν, ἔφη, ὑμῖν δοκεῖ μαστροποῦ ἔργον
εἶναι ἢν ἂν ἢ ὃν ἂν μαστροπεύῃ ἀρέσκοντα
τοῦτον ἀποδεικνύναι οἷς ἂν συνῇ ; Πάνυ
μὲν οὖν, ἔφασαν. Οὐκοῦν ἓν μέν τί ἐστιν
εἰς τὸ ἀρέσκειν ἐκ τοῦ πρέπουσαν ἔχειν σχέ-
σιν καὶ τριχῶν καὶ ἐσθῆτος ; Πάνυ μὲν
οὖν, ἔφασαν. Οὐκοῦν καὶ τόδε ἐπιστάμεθα 58
ὅτι ἔστιν ἀνθρώπῳ τοῖς αὐτοῖς ὄμμασι καὶ
φιλικῶς καὶ ἐχθρῶς πρός τινας βλέπειν ;
Πάνυ μὲν οὖν. Τί δέ, τῇ αὐτῇ φωνῇ ἔστι
καὶ αἰδημόνως καὶ θρασέως φθέγγεσθαι ;
Πάνυ μὲν οὖν. Τί δέ, λόγοι οὐκ εἰσὶ μέν
τινες ἀπεχθανόμενοι, εἰσὶ δέ τινες οἳ πρὸς
φιλίαν ἄγουσι ; Πάνυ μὲν οὖν. Οὐκοῦν τού- 59
των ὁ ἀγαθὸς μαστροπὸς τὰ συμφέροντα εἰς
τὸ ἀρέσκειν διδάσκοι ἄν ; Πάνυ μὲν οὖν.

Ἀμείνων δ᾿ ἂν εἴη, ἔφη, ὁ ἑνὶ δυνάμενος ἀρε-
στοὺς ποιεῖν ἢ ὅστις καὶ πολλοῖς ; ἐνταῦθα
μέντοι ἐσχίσθησαν, καὶ οἱ μὲν εἶπον Δῆλον
60 ὅτι ὅστις πλείστοις, οἱ δὲ Πάνυ μὲν οὖν. ὁ
δ᾿ εἰπὼν ὅτι καὶ τοῦτο ὁμολογεῖται ἔφη, εἰ
δέ τις καὶ ὅλῃ τῇ πόλει ἀρέσκοντας δύναιτο
ἀποδεικνύναι, οὐχ οὗτος παντελῶς ἂν ἤδη
ἀγαθὸς μαστροπὸς εἴη ; Σαφῶς γε νὴ Δία,
πάντες εἶπον. Οὐκοῦν εἴ τις τοιούτους δύναιτο
ἐξεργάζεσθαι ὧν προστατοίη, δικαίως ἂν μέγα
φρονοίη ἐπὶ τῇ τέχνῃ καὶ δικαίως ἂν πολὺν
61 μισθὸν λαμβάνοι ; ἐπεὶ δὲ καὶ ταῦτα πάντες
συνωμολόγουν, Τοιοῦτος μέντοι, ἔφη, μοι δοκεῖ
Ἀντισθένης εἶναι οὗτος. καὶ ὁ Ἀντισθένης,
Ἐμοί, ἔφη, παραδίδως, ὦ Σώκρατες, τὴν
τέχνην ; Ναὶ μὰ Δί᾿, ἔφη. ὁρῶ γάρ σε καὶ
τὴν ἀκόλουθον ταύτης πάνυ ἐξειργασμένον.
62 Τίνα ταύτην ; Τὴν προαγωγείαν, ἔφη. καὶ
ὃς μάλα ἀχθεσθεὶς ἐπήρετο, Καὶ τί μοι
σύνοισθα, ὦ Σώκρατες, τοιοῦτον εἰργασμένῳ ;
Οἶδα μέν, ἔφη, σε Καλλίαν τουτονὶ προαγω-
γεύσαντα τῷ σοφῷ Προδίκῳ, ὅτε ἑώρας τοῦτον μὲν φιλοσοφίας ἐρῶντα, ἐκεῖνον δὲ χρημάτων δεόμενον· οἶδα δέ σε Ἱππίᾳ τῷ
Ἠλείῳ, παρ᾿ οὗ οὗτος καὶ τὸ μνημονικὸν ἔμα-
θεν· ἀφ᾿ οὗ δὴ καὶ ἐρωτικώτερος γεγένηται
διὰ τὸ ὅ τι ἂν καλὸν ἴδῃ μηδέποτε ἐπιλαν-
63 θάνεσθαι. ἔναγχος δὲ δήπου καὶ πρὸς ἐμὲ

ἐπαινῶν τὸν Ἡρακλεώτην ξένον ἐπεί με ἐποί-
ησας ἐπιθυμεῖν αὐτοῦ, συνέστησάς μοι αὐτόν.
καὶ χάριν μέντοι σοι ἔχω· πάνυ γὰρ καλὸς
κἀγαθὸς δοκεῖ μοι εἶναι. Αἰσχύλον δὲ τὸν
Φλιάσιον πρὸς ἐμὲ ἐπαινῶν καὶ ἐμὲ πρὸς
ἐκεῖνον οὐχ οὕτω διέθηκας ὥστε διὰ τοὺς
σοὺς λόγους ἐρῶντες ἐκυνοδρομοῦμεν ἀλλήλους
ζητοῦντες; ταῦτα οὖν ὁρῶν δυνάμενόν σε 64
ποιεῖν ἀγαθὸν νομίζω προαγωγὸν εἶναι. ὁ γὰρ
οἷός τε ὢν γιγνώσκειν τε τοὺς ὠφελίμους
αὐτοῖς καὶ τούτους δυνάμενος ποιεῖν ἐπιθυμεῖν ἀλλήλων, οὗτος ἄν μοι δοκεῖ καὶ πόλεις
δύνασθαι φίλας ποιεῖν καὶ γάμους ἐπιτηδείους
συνάγειν, καὶ πολλοῦ ἂν ἄξιος εἶναι καὶ
πόλεσι καὶ φίλοις καὶ συμμάχοις κεκτῆσθαι.
σὺ δὲ ὡς κακῶς ἀκούσας ὅτι ἀγαθόν σε ἔφην
προαγωγὸν εἶναι, ὠργίσθης. Ἀλλὰ μὰ Δί',
ἔφη, οὐ νῦν. ἐὰν γὰρ ταῦτα δύνωμαι, σεσαγμένος δὴ παντάπασι πλούτου τὴν ψυχὴν
ἔσομαι. καὶ αὕτη μὲν δὴ ἡ περίοδος τῶν
λόγων ἀπετελέσθη.

fable talk

CHAPTER V.

The contest of beauty between Socrates and Critobulus.

Ὁ δὲ Καλλίας ἔφη, Σὺ δὲ δή, ὦ Κριτό- 1
βουλε, εἰς τὸν περὶ τοῦ κάλλους ἀγῶνα πρὸς
Σωκράτην οὐκ ἀνθίστασαι; Νὴ Δί', ἔφη ὁ

Σωκράτης, ἴσως γὰρ εὐδοκιμοῦντα τὸν μαστρο-
2 πὸν παρὰ τοῖς κριταῖς ὁρᾷ. Ἀλλ' ὅμως,
ἔφη ὁ Κριτόβουλος, οὐκ ἀναδύομαι· ἀλλὰ
δίδασκε, εἴ τι ἔχεις σοφόν, ὡς καλλίων εἶ
ἐμοῦ. μόνον, ἔφη, τὸν λαμπτῆρα ἐγγὺς προσ-
ενεγκάτω. Εἰς ἀνάκρισιν τοίνυν σε, ἔφη,
πρῶτον τῆς δίκης καλοῦμαι· ἀλλ' ἀποκρίνου.
3 Σὺ δέ γε ἐρώτα. Πότερον οὖν ἐν ἀνθρώπῳ
μόνον νομίζεις τὸ καλὸν εἶναι ἢ καὶ ἐν ἄλλῳ
τινί; Ἐγὼ μὲν ναὶ μὰ Δί', ἔφη, καὶ ἐν ἵππῳ
καὶ βοῒ καὶ ἐν ἀψύχοις πολλοῖς. οἶδα γοῦν
οὖσαν καὶ ἀσπίδα καλὴν καὶ ξίφος καὶ δόρυ.
4 Καὶ πῶς, ἔφη, οἷόν τε ταῦτα μηδὲν ὅμοια
ὄντα ἀλλήλοις πάντα καλὰ εἶναι; Ἢν νὴ
Δί', ἔφη, πρὸς τὰ ἔργα ὧν ἕνεκα ἕκαστα
κτώμεθα εὖ εἰργασμένα ᾖ ἢ εὖ πεφυκότα
πρὸς ἃ ἂν δεώμεθα, καὶ ταῦτ', ἔφη ὁ Κριτό-
5 βουλος, καλά. Οἶσθα οὖν, ἔφη, ὀφθαλμῶν
τίνος ἕνεκα δεόμεθα; Δῆλον, ἔφη, ὅτι τοῦ
ὁρᾶν. Οὕτω μὲν τοίνυν ἤδη οἱ ἐμοὶ ὀφθαλ-
μοὶ καλλίονες ἂν τῶν σῶν εἴησαν. Πῶς δή;
Ὅτι οἱ μὲν σοὶ τὸ κατ' εὐθὺ μόνον ὁρῶσιν,
οἱ δὲ ἐμοὶ καὶ τὸ ἐκ πλαγίου διὰ τὸ ἐπιπό-
λαιοι εἶναι. Λέγεις σύ, ἔφη, καρκίνον εὐοφθαλ-
μότατον εἶναι τῶν ζῴων; Πάντως δήπου,
ἔφη· ἐπεὶ καὶ πρὸς ἰσχὺν τοὺς ὀφθαλμοὺς
6 ἄριστα πεφυκότας ἔχει. Εἶεν, ἔφη, τῶν δὲ
ῥινῶν ποτέρα καλλίων, ἡ σὴ ἢ ἡ ἐμή; Ἐγὼ

μέν, ἔφη, οἶμαι τὴν ἐμήν, εἴπερ γε τοῦ
ὀσφραίνεσθαι ἕνεκεν ἐποίησαν ἡμῖν ῥῖνας οἱ
θεοί. οἱ μὲν γὰρ σοὶ μυκτῆρες εἰς γῆν ὁρῶσιν, οἱ δὲ ἐμοὶ ἀναπέπτανται, ὥστε τὰς πάν-
τοθεν ὀσμὰς προσδέχεσθαι. Τὸ δὲ δὴ σιμὸν
τῆς ῥινὸς πῶς τοῦ ὀρθοῦ κάλλιον; Ὅτι, ἔφη,
οὐκ ἀντιφράττει, ἀλλ᾽ ἐᾷ εὐθὺς τὰς ὄψεις
ὁρᾶν ἃ ἂν βούλωνται· ἡ δὲ ὑψηλὴ ῥὶς ὥσπερ
ἐπηρεάζουσα διατετείχικε τὰ ὄμματα. Τοῦ 7
γε μὴν στόματος, ἔφη ὁ Κριτόβουλος, ὑφίε-
μαι. εἰ γὰρ τοῦ ἀποδάκνειν ἕνεκα πεποίηται,
πολὺ ἂν σὺ μεῖζον ἢ ἐγὼ ἀποδάκοις. Διὰ δὲ τὸ
παχέα ἔχειν τὰ χείλη οὐκ οἴει καὶ μαλακώτε-
ρόν σου ἔχειν τὸ φίλημα; Ἔοικα, ἔφη, ἐγὼ
κατὰ τὸν σὸν λόγον καὶ τῶν ὄνων αἴσχιον τὸ
στόμα ἔχειν. Ἐκεῖνο δὲ οὐδὲν τεκμήριον λογί-
ζει ὡς ἐγὼ σοῦ καλλίων εἰμί, ὅτι καὶ Ναΐδες
θεαὶ οὖσαι τοὺς Σειληνοὺς ἐμοὶ ὁμοιοτέρους
τίκτουσιν ἢ σοί; καὶ ὁ Κριτόβουλος, Οὐκέτι, 8
ἔφη, ἔχω πρὸς σὲ ἀντιλέγειν, ἀλλὰ διαφερόντων, ἔφη, τὰς ψήφους, ἵνα ὡς τάχιστα εἰδῶ
ὅ τι με χρὴ παθεῖν ἢ ἀποτῖσαι. μόνον, ἔφη,
κρυφῇ φερόντων· δέδοικα γὰρ τὸν σὸν καὶ
Ἀντισθένους πλοῦτον μὴ με καταδυναστεύσῃ.
ἡ μὲν δὴ παῖς καὶ ὁ παῖς κρύφα ἀνέφερον. 9
ὁ δὲ Σωκράτης ἐν τούτῳ διέπραττε τόν τε
λύχνον ἀντιπροσενεγκεῖν τῷ Κριτοβούλῳ, ὡς
μὴ ἐξαπατηθεῖσαν οἱ κριταί, καὶ τῷ νικη-

σαντι μὴ ταινίας ἀλλὰ φιλήματα ἀναδήματα
10 παρὰ τῶν κριτῶν γενέσθαι. ἐπεὶ δὲ ἐξέπεσον αἱ ψῆφοι καὶ ἐγένοντο πᾶσαι σὺν Κριτοβούλῳ, Παπαῖ, ἔφη ὁ Σωκράτης, οὐχ ὅμοιον
ἔοικε τὸ σὸν ἀργύριον, ὦ Κριτόβουλε, τῷ
Καλλίου εἶναι. τὸ μὲν γὰρ τούτου δικαιοτέρους ποιεῖ, τὸ δὲ σὸν ὥσπερ τὸ πλεῖστον
διαφθείρειν ἱκανόν ἐστι καὶ δικαστὰς καὶ
κριτάς.

CHAPTER VI.

Socrates' conversation engrosses attention : the Syracusan is vexed, and becomes impertinent.

1 Ἐκ δὲ τούτου οἱ μὲν τὰ νικητήρια φιλήματα ἀπολαμβάνειν τὸν Κριτόβουλον ἐκέλευον, οἱ δὲ τὸν κύριον πείθειν, οἱ δὲ καὶ ἄλλα
ἔσκωπτον. ὁ δὲ Ἑρμογένης κἀνταῦθα ἐσιώπα.
καὶ ὁ Σωκράτης ὀνομάσας αὐτόν, Ἔχοις ἄν,
ἔφη, ὦ Ἑρμόγενες, εἰπεῖν ἡμῖν τί ἐστι παροινία ; καὶ ὃς ἀπεκρίνατο, Εἰ μὲν ὅ τι ἐστὶν
ἐρωτᾷς, οὐκ οἶδα· τὸ μέντοι μοι δοκοῦν
2 εἴποιμ' ἄν. Ἀλλ' ὃ δοκεῖ, τοῦτ', ἔφη. Τὸ
τοίνυν παρ' οἶνον λυπεῖν τοὺς συνόντας, τοῦτ'
ἐγὼ κρίνω παροινίαν. Οἶσθ' οὖν, ἔφη, ὅτι
καὶ σὺ νῦν ἡμᾶς λυπεῖς σιωπῶν ; Ἢ καὶ
ὅταν λέγῃτ' ; ἔφη. Οὔκ, ἀλλ' ὅταν διαλίπω-

μεν. Ἦ οὖν λέληθέ σε ὅτι μεταξὺ τοῦ ὑμᾶς
λέγειν οὐδ᾽ ἂν τρίχα, μὴ ὅτι λόγον ἄν τις
παρείρειε; καὶ ὁ Σωκράτης, Ὦ Καλλία, ἔχοις 3
ἄν τι, ἔφη, ἀνδρὶ ἐλεγχομένῳ βοηθῆσαι;
Ἔγωγ᾽, ἔφη. ὅταν γὰρ ὁ αὐλὸς φθέγγηται,
παντάπασι σιωπῶμεν. καὶ ὁ Ἑρμογένης,
Ἦ οὖν βούλεσθε, ἔφη, ὥσπερ Νικόστρατος
ὁ ὑποκριτὴς τετράμετρα πρὸς τὸν αὐλὸν κατέ-
λεγεν, οὕτω καὶ ὑπὸ τοῦ αὐλοῦ ὑμῖν διαλέγωμαι; καὶ ὁ Σωκράτης, Πρὸς τῶν θεῶν, 4
ἔφη, Ἑρμόγενες, οὕτω ποίει. οἶμαι γάρ,
ὥσπερ ἡ ᾠδὴ ἡδίων πρὸς τὸν αὐλόν, οὕτω
καὶ τοὺς σοὺς λόγους ἡδύνεσθαι ἄν τι ὑπὸ
τῶν φθόγγων, ἄλλως τε καὶ εἰ μορφάζοις
ὥσπερ ἡ αὐλητρὶς καὶ σὺ πρὸς τὰ λεγόμενα.
καὶ ὁ Καλλίας ἔφη, Ὅταν οὖν ὁ Ἀντισθένης 5
ὅδ᾽ ἐλέγχῃ τινὰ ἐν τῷ συμποσίῳ, τί ἔσται τὸ
αὔλημα; καὶ ὁ Ἀντισθένης εἶπε, Τῷ μὲν
ἐλεγχομένῳ οἶμαι ἄν, ἔφη, πρέπειν συριγμόν.

Τοιούτων δὲ λόγων ὄντων ὡς ἑώρα ὁ Συρα- 6
κόσιος τῶν μὲν αὑτοῦ ἐπιδειγμάτων ἀμελοῦν-
τας, ἀλλήλοις δὲ ἡδομένους, φθονῶν τῷ
Σωκράτει εἶπεν, Ἆρα σύ, ὦ Σώκρατες, ὁ
φροντιστὴς ἐπικαλούμενος; Οὔκουν κάλλιον,
ἔφη, ἢ εἰ ἀφρόντιστος ἐκαλούμην; Εἰ μή
γε ἐδόκεις τῶν μετεώρων φροντιστὴς εἶναι.
Οἶσθα οὖν, ἔφη ὁ Σωκράτης, μετεωρότερόν 7
τι τῶν θεῶν; Ἀλλ᾽ οὐ μὰ Δί᾽, ἔφη, οὐ

36 ΞΕΝΟΦΩΝΤΟΣ

τούτων σε λέγουσιν ἐπιμελεῖσθαι, ἀλλὰ τῶν
ἄνω ἐν νεφέλαις ὄντων. Οὐκοῦν καὶ οὕτως
ἄν, ἔφη, θεῶν ἐπιμελοίμην· ἄνωθεν μέν γε
ὕοντες ὠφελοῦσιν, ἄνωθεν δὲ φῶς παρέχουσιν.
εἰ δὲ ψυχρὰ λέγω, σὺ αἴτιος, ἔφη, πράγματά
8 μοι παρέχων. Ταῦτα μέν, ἔφη, ἔα· ἀλλ᾽
εἰπέ μοι πόσους ψύλλης πόδας ἐμοῦ ἀπέχεις.
ταῦτα γάρ σέ φασι γεωμετρεῖν. καὶ ὁ Ἀντισθένης εἶπε, Σὺ μέντοι δεινὸς εἶ, ὦ Φίλιππε,
εἰκάζειν. οὐ δοκεῖ σοι ὁ ἀνὴρ οὗτος λοιδο-
ρεῖσθαι βουλομένῳ ἐοικέναι; Ναὶ μὰ τὸν
9 Δί᾽, ἔφη, καὶ ἄλλοις γε πολλοῖς. Ἀλλ᾽
ὅμως, ἔφη ὁ Σωκράτης, σὺ αὐτὸν μὴ εἴκαζε,
ἵνα μὴ καὶ σὺ λοιδορουμένῳ ἐοίκῃς. Ἀλλ᾽
εἴπερ γε τοῖς πᾶσι καλοῖς καὶ τοῖς βελτί-
στοις εἰκάζω αὐτόν, ἐπαινοῦντι μᾶλλον ἢ
λοιδορουμένῳ δικαίως ἂν εἰκάζοι μέ τις. Καὶ
νῦν σύγε λοιδορουμένῳ ἔοικας, εἰ πάντ᾽ αὐτοῦ
10 βελτίω φῇς εἶναι. Ἀλλὰ βούλει πονηροτέροις
εἰκάζω αὐτόν; Μηδὲ πονηροτέροις. Ἀλλὰ
μηδενί; Μηδενὶ μηδὲν τοῦτον εἴκαζε. Ἀλλ᾽
οὐ μέντοι γε σιωπῶν οἶδα ὅπως ἄξια τοῦ
δείπνου ἐργάσομαι. Καὶ ῥᾳδίως γ᾽, ἂν ἃ μὴ
δεῖ λέγειν, ἔφη, σιωπᾷς. αὕτη μὲν δὴ ἡ
παροινία οὕτω κατεσβέσθη.

CHAPTER VII.

Socrates objects to perilous and senseless performances
by the dancers.

Ἐκ τούτου δὲ τῶν ἄλλων οἱ μὲν ἐκέλευον 1
εἰκάζειν, οἱ δὲ ἐκώλυον. θορύβου δὲ ὄντος
ὁ Σωκράτης αὖ πάλιν εἶπεν, Ἄρα ἐπειδὴ
πάντες ἐπιθυμοῦμεν λέγειν, νῦν ἂν μάλιστα
καὶ ἅμα ᾄσαιμεν; καὶ εὐθὺς τοῦτ' εἰπὼν
ἦρχεν ᾠδῆς. ἐπεὶ δ' ἦσαν, εἰσεφέρετο τῇ 2
ὀρχηστρίδι τροχὸς τῶν κεραμικῶν, ἐφ' οὗ
ἔμελλε θαυματουργήσειν. ἔνθα δὴ εἶπεν ὁ
Σωκράτης, Ὦ Συρακόσιε, κινδυνεύω ἐγώ,
ὥσπερ σὺ λέγεις, τῷ ὄντι φροντιστὴς εἶναι·
νῦν γοῦν σκοπῶ ὅπως ἂν ὁ μὲν παῖς ὅδε ὁ
σὸς καὶ ἡ παῖς ἥδε ὡς ῥᾷστα διάγοιεν, ἡμεῖς
δὲ μάλιστ' ἂν εὐφραινοίμεθα θεώμενοι αὐτούς·
ὅπερ εὖ οἶδα ὅτι καὶ σὺ βούλει. δοκεῖ οὖν 3
μοι τὸ μὲν εἰς μαχαίρας κυβιστᾶν κινδύνου
ἐπίδειγμα εἶναι, ὃ συμποσίῳ οὐδὲν προσήκει.
καὶ μὴν τό γε ἐπὶ τοῦ τροχοῦ ἅμα περιδι-
νουμένου γράφειν τε καὶ ἀναγιγνώσκειν θαῦμα
μὲν ἴσως τί ἐστιν, ἡδονὴν δὲ οὐδὲ ταῦτα
δύναμαι γνῶναι τίν' ἂν παράσχοι. οὐδὲ μὴν
τό γε διαστρέφοντας τὰ σώματα καὶ τροχοὺς
μιμουμένους ἥδιον ἢ ἡσυχίαν ἔχοντας τοὺς
καλοὺς καὶ ὡραίους θεωρεῖν. καὶ γὰρ δὴ οὐδὲ 4
πάνυ τι σπάνιον τό γε θαυμασίοις ἐντυχεῖν,

εἴ τις τούτου δεῖται, ἀλλ᾽ ἔξεστιν αὐτίκα
μάλα τὰ παρόντα θαυμάζειν, τί ποτε ὁ μὲν
λύχνος διὰ τὸ λαμπρὰν φλόγα ἔχειν φῶς
παρέχει, τὸ δὲ χαλκεῖον λαμπρὸν ὂν φῶς
μὲν οὐ ποιεῖ, ἐν αὑτῷ δὲ ἄλλα ἐμφαινόμενα
παρέχεται· καὶ πῶς τὸ μὲν ἔλαιον ὑγρὸν ὂν
αὔξει τὴν φλόγα, τὸ δὲ ὕδωρ, ὅτι ὑγρόν ἐστι,
κατασβέννυσι τὸ πῦρ. ἀλλὰ γὰρ καὶ ταῦτα
5 μὲν οὐκ εἰς ταὐτὸν τῷ οἴνῳ ἐπισπεύδει· εἰ
δὲ ὀρχοῖντο πρὸς τὸν αὐλὸν σχήματα ἐν οἷς
Χάριτές τε καὶ Ὧραι καὶ Νύμφαι γράφονται,
πολὺ ἂν οἶμαι αὐτούς τε ῥᾷον διάγειν καὶ
τὸ συμπόσιον πολὺ ἐπιχαριτώτερον εἶναι.
ὁ οὖν Συρακόσιος, Ἀλλὰ ναὶ μὰ τὸν Δί᾽,
ἔφη, ὦ Σώκρατες, καλῶς τε λέγεις καὶ ἐγὼ
εἰσάξω θεάματα ἐφ᾽ οἷς ὑμεῖς εὐφρανεῖσθε.
Ὁ μὲν δὴ Συρακόσιος ἐξελθὼν συνεκροτεῖτο·
ὁ δὲ Σωκράτης πάλιν αὖ καινοῦ λόγου
κατῆρχεν.

———◆———

[CHAPTER VIII., *here omitted, is chiefly a monologue.
Socrates is therein made to deliver a long and
earnestly meant disquisition on Love. Alluding
to the dual Aphrodite, he distinguishes carnal
passion from the affection based on noble qualities
of mind and heart. With no little pleasantry he
rebukes sharply the vices which the former fos-
ters, and eloquently extols the latter as god-like
and ennobling.*]

CHAPTER IX.

The banquet concludes with a ballet, representing the loves
of Dionysus and Ariadne.

Οὗτος μὲν δὴ ὁ λόγος ἐνταῦθα ἔληξεν. 1
Αὐτόλυκος δέ, ἤδη γὰρ ὥρα ἦν αὐτῷ, ἐξανί-
στατο εἰς περίπατον· καὶ ὁ Λύκων ὁ πατὴρ
αὐτῷ συνεξιὼν ἐπιστραφεὶς εἶπε, Νὴ τὴν
Ἥραν, ὦ Σώκρατες, καλός γε κἀγαθὸς δοκεῖς
μοι ἄνθρωπος εἶναι.

Ἐκ δὲ τούτου πρῶτον μὲν θρόνος τις 2
ἔνδον κατετέθη, ἔπειτα δὲ ὁ Συρακόσιος εἰσελ-
θὼν εἶπεν, Ὦ ἄνδρες, Ἀριάδνη εἴσεισιν εἰς
τὸν ἑαυτῆς τε καὶ Διονύσου θάλαμον· μετὰ
δὲ τοῦθ᾽ ἥξει Διόνυσος ὑποπεπωκὼς παρὰ
θεοῖς καὶ εἴσεισι πρὸς αὐτήν, ἔπειτα παι-
ξοῦνται πρὸς ἀλλήλους. ἐκ τούτου πρῶτον 3
μὲν ἡ Ἀριάδνη ὡς νύμφη κεκοσμημένη παρ-
ῆλθε καὶ ἐκαθέζετο ἐπὶ τοῦ θρόνου. οὔπω
δὲ φαινομένου τοῦ Διονύσου ηὐλεῖτο ὁ βακ-
χεῖος ῥυθμός. ἔνθα δὴ ἠγάσθησαν τὸν ὀρχη-
στοδιδάσκαλον. εὐθὺς μὲν γὰρ ἡ Ἀριάδνη
ἀκούσασα τοιοῦτόν τι ἐποίησεν ὡς πᾶς ἂν
ἔγνω ὅτι ἀσμένη ἤκουσε· καὶ ὑπήντησε μὲν
οὐ οὐδὲ ἀνέστη, δήλη δ᾽ ἦν μόλις ἠρεμοῦσα.
ἐπεί γε μὴν κατεῖδεν αὐτὴν ὁ Διόνυσος, ἐπι- 4
χορεύσας ὥσπερ ἂν εἴ τις φιλικώτατα ἐκαθέ-

ζετο ἐπὶ τῶν γονάτων, καὶ περιλαβὼν ἐφίλησεν αὐτήν. ἡ δ' αἰδουμένη μὲν ἐῴκει,
ὅμως δὲ φιλικῶς ἀντιπεριελάμβανεν. οἱ δὲ
συμπόται ὁρῶντες ἅμα μὲν ἐκρότουν, ἅμα δὲ
5 ἐβόων αὖθις. ὡς δὲ ὁ Διόνυσος ἀνιστάμενος
συνανέστησε μεθ' ἑαυτοῦ τὴν Ἀριάδνην, ἐκ
τούτου δὴ φιλούντων τε καὶ ἀσπαζομένων
ἀλλήλους σχήματα παρῆν θεάσασθαι. οἱ δ'
ὁρῶντες ὄντως καλὸν μὲν τὸν Διόνυσον,
ὡραίαν δὲ τὴν Ἀριάδνην, οὐ σκώπτοντας δὲ
ἀλλ' ἀληθινῶς τοῖς στόμασι φιλοῦντας, πάντες
6 ἀνεπτερωμένοι ἐθεῶντο. καὶ γὰρ ἤκουον τοῦ
Διονύσου μὲν ἐπερωτῶντος αὐτὴν εἰ φιλεῖ
αὐτόν, τῆς δ' οὕτως ἐπομνυούσης ὥστε μὴ
μόνον τὸν Διόνυσον ἀλλὰ καὶ τοὺς παρόντας
ἅπαντας συνομόσαι ἂν ἦ μὴν τὸν παῖδα καὶ
τὴν παῖδα ὑπ' ἀλλήλων φιλεῖσθαι. ἐῴκεσαν
γὰρ οὐ δεδιδαγμένοις τὰ σχήματα ἀλλ' ἐφειμένοις πράττειν ἃ πάλαι ἐπεθύμουν.

7 Τέλος δὲ οἱ συμπόται ἰδόντες, οἱ μὲν ἄγα-
μοι γαμεῖν ἐπώμνυσαν, οἱ δὲ γεγαμηκότες
ἀναβάντες ἐπὶ τοὺς ἵππους ἀπήλαυνον πρὸς
τοὺς ἑαυτῶν οἴκους. Σωκράτης δὲ καὶ τῶν
ἄλλων οἱ ὑπομείναντες πρὸς Λύκωνα καὶ
τὸν υἱὸν σὺν Καλλίᾳ περιπατήσοντες ἀπῆλ-
θον. αὕτη τοῦ τότε συμποσίου κατάλυσις
ἐγένετο.

NOTES.

NOTES.

———•◦•———

THE SYMPOSIUM here described is represented as occur-
ring in the year 422 B.C. The scene is laid at the house
of Callias in the Piræus. The *dramatis personæ* are as
follows : —

CALLIAS, the host. He came of an old and distinguished
family ; the office of *Daduchus*, or Torchbearer, in the
Eleusinian mysteries was an hereditary honor belonging to
it. He was about 25 at this time, and only recently had
inherited the immense wealth of his father, Hipponicus,
reputed to have been the richest Greek of his day. The
scene of Plato's *Protagoras* is also laid at his house :
οἶκος τῆς πόλεως ὁ μέγιστος καὶ ὀλβιώτατος — is a com-
pliment uttered on that occasion. By extravagance and
loose living he squandered his estate, dying in poverty.
See Athenæus XII. lii ; Lysias, *de Bon. Arist.* 48. This
Callias appears thrice in political history : as active in the
prosecution of Andocides, 400 B.C. (Andoc. *de Myst.* 15,
(112) *sqq.*) ; as commander of the hoplites in the affair
with the Spartans at Corinth, 392 (Xen. *Hellen.* IV. v.
13) ; and as peace commissioner to Sparta, 371 (*Hellen.*
VI. iii). The speech which Xenophon gives him on the
latter occasion is vain, bombastic, and superficial.

AUTOLYCUS, in whose honor the banquet is given. Pausanias remarks a statue of Autolycus, ὁ παγκρατιαστής,
in the Prytaneum : I. xviii. 3, and IX. xxxii. 8. Pliny,

H. N. XXXIV. xix. 17, further mentions Leochares as the artist. Autolycus was put to death by the Thirty in 404 : Diod. XIV. v. 7.

LYCON, known only as the father of the preceding.

NICERATUS, a wealthy friend of Callias. His father was Nicias, noted for his large fortune, and a distinguished general and statesman during the Peloponnesian war. Niceratus' wealth led to his untimely death : he was proscribed by the Thirty. *Hellen.* II. iii. 39 ; also Lysias, XVIII. 6, *contra Poliochum.*

SOCRATES, — already a well-known public character. Upon the crowded thoroughfare and in shop and stithy was to be seen his burly figure. His uncouth features, so out of keeping with his interior worth and refinement, made his conversation a constant surprise, as he charmed men with his genial humor, his kindly admonitions, and his intellectual suggestiveness. Socrates was the prince of good talkers : his style was simple and plain, his manner uniformly suave, yet, as Eupolis said of Pericles, his words always 'left their sting infixed,' — acting as a healthful spur to some, in others causing a rankling sore. So Socrates had enemies. Doubtless he had already conceived his great mission, to elevate men morally, and was known to have some new ideas. Indeed, two years previous Aristophanes — with much wit and little justice — had set him off before a crowded theatre as a pronounced sceptic ; and hence, as we shall see, suspicions of his orthodoxy were prevalent.

ANTISTHENES, a devoted follower of Socrates. He received his early training from Gorgias. He here exhibits his reputed keenness in debate, together with much of the irrepressible, contradictious spirit of the professional sophist. After Socrates' death he founded the Cynic school, advocating the unity of God ; virtue as the paramount good, — all pleasures of sense to be contemned.

HERMOGENES, a younger brother of Callias, but apparently inheriting no share of their father's wealth. Even more notable than his poverty are his modesty and his piety : in modern times this younger son would have taken sacred orders. In *Mem.* II. x. Socrates commends him to Diodorus as a deserving man who would make a valuable friend. He is mentioned also in *Mem.* IV. viii. 4; and is a character in Plato's *Cratylus.*

CRITOBULUS, the son of Socrates' patron and intimate friend, Crito. He was talented, and handsome, but vain. Socrates holds dialogue with him in *Mem.* II. vi.

CHARMIDES was a cousin of the notorious Critias, and an uncle of Plato; a young man of fine parts, and modest even to diffidence. See Socrates' conversation with him, *Mem.* III. vii. He was made governor of the Piræus under the Thirty, and fell in the engagement which accomplished their overthrow. Plato names a dialogue after him.

PHILIPPUS, a professional jester, who forces himself upon the company.

A *Syracusan,* a strolling showman; accompanied by two girls and a boy. These entertain the guests with music and mimetic dances.

CHAPTER I.

1 1. 'Αλλ' ἐμοὶ δοκεῖ, 'I hold,' 'in my opinion.' It is
characteristic of Greek discourse to formally connect every
sentence with the preceding. ἀλλά is used for abrupt
transitions, often where English idiom uses no connective ;
sometimes our resumptive 'well' may conventionally represent it.

This abrupt introduction, as well as the opening statement itself, shows that the SYMPOSIUM was intended as a
companion piece to the *Œconomicus* and the *Memorabilia* ;
in the latter of which Xenophon gives faithful recollections
of his master's life and doctrine, and in the former takes
Socrates as an ideal philosopher through whom to set forth
his own views on Domestic Economy.   Here Xenophon
presents another aspect of Socrates' character, his wit and
his infinite *bonhomie* ; and at the same time he pictures a
typical Athenian dinner party.

Xenophon has elsewhere given more or less extended
accounts of banquets : thus, *Cyrop.* I. iii. 4–12, II. ii, V. ii.
14–20, VIII. iv. 1–27 ; *Anab.* VI. i. 3–13, VII. iii. 15–34 ;
Mem. III. xiv.

καλῶν κἀγαθῶν, 'great and good.' This phrase represents the Greek ideal of character and worth : translate
it variously, 'the *good* man,' 'the true gentleman,' 'the
man of culture,' etc.

ἐ. τ. παιδιαῖς, 'in their merry moods.'

οἷς παραγενόμενος, 'an affair at which I was present' :
probably not to be taken literally, but with novelist's
license. Xenophon would have been too young (about
10) ; and otherwise, it is unlikely that he would have given

himself no part in the after proceedings. Plato, on the other hand, less dramatically conceives his Symposium in the third person, as reported by one present to a friend, and by him retold to still another.

ταῦτα γιγνώσκ. is 'hold this opinion.'

2. Παναθηναίων. The "greater" Panathenæa was celebrated in the third year of each olympiad. There was a "lesser" in the other years. This festival in honor of Pallas Athena was of very ancient origin. It was celebrated with great magnificence by sacrifices, games and all sorts of contests, literary recitations, musical competition, and the like. Its distinctive feature was a grand procession, in which almost the entire population took part, nominally to carry the *peplos* of the Goddess to her shrine on the Acropolis.

ἐρῶν ἐτύγχ., 'was a fond admirer.'

νενικ. – παγκράτιον, 'recently victor in the *pancratium*.' The *pancratium*, the severest of the contests, consisted of a union of boxing and wrestling; great license of attack was allowed, but attempts to maim simply were ruled out. There were separate contests for boys. For the case, G.* 1052; H. 716. *a.*

Πειραιεῖ. The Piræus was the seaport of Athens, 4½ miles distant, and connected by the famous long walls. Many wealthy Athenians had houses there overlooking the sea.

3. ὁμοῦ ὄντας, 'in a group.' —— τοῖς ἀμφὶ Σ., 'Socrates and his companions' : so this idiom everywhere.

4. εἰς καλόν γε, 'it is very fortunate.' Cf. εἰς καλὸν ἥκεις, Pl. *Symp.* 174 E.

ἑστιᾶν, 'entertain.' The verb is denominative from ἑστία, 'hearth.'

ἀν – φανῆναι, εἰ – εἴη: G. 1408, 1483.

---

* G. = Goodwin's Greek Grammar, rev. ed., 1892 ; H = Hadley-Allen, 1884; GMT. = Goodwin's Moods and Tenses, 1890.

εἰ . . . κεκοσμημένος, 'if my halls were graced with the presence of men of cultivated minds.'

ἀνδρῶν, properly 'the men's apartments,' as opposed to γυναικών, 'the women's apartments'; here, as commonly, used of the guest rooms. This suffix -ών denotes place; so ἱππών is 'a horse-stable,' ἀμπελών, 'a vineyard.'

σπουδαρχίαις, 'office-seekers.'

5. Πρωταγόρᾳ, κ. τ. λ.: noted Sophists. **Protagoras**, from Abdera, taught rhetoric; he philosophized also on metaphysical problems. With him truth was subjective and relative: πάντων χρημάτων μέτρον ἐστὶν ἄνθρωπος, τῶν μὲν ὄντων ὡς ἔστι, τῶν δὲ οὐκ ὄντων ὡς οὐκ ἔστιν, is his famous dictum. In theology he was an agnostic. He would neither affirm nor deny the existence of Gods: the matter is obscure, and life all too short to settle it.

Gorgias, of Leontini, was a very celebrated rhetorician. In philosophy he was a thorough-going agnostic, a nihilist: nothing exists, and if so, all knowledge of it were impossible; persuasion is everything, and rhetoric is πειθοῦς δημιουργός.

Prodicus discoursed largely on ethical subjects; ὁ σοφός is his habitual epithet. His apologue of Heracles at the Road-forks Xenophon puts into the mouth of Socrates, *Mem.* II. i. 21 *sqq.* He was wont in defence of his vocation to quote Epicharmus' aphorism, ἁ δὲ χεὶρ τὰν χεῖρα νίζει· δός τι, καὶ λάβοις τί κα, frag. 118 (Aehrens). —— HIPPIAS and EVENUS were other noted teachers, known to have instructed Callias. Cf. *infra* iv. 62; and Pl. *Apol.* 20 A-C, where Socrates says of Callias: τετέλεκε χρήματα σοφισταῖς πλείω ἢ ξύμπαντες οἱ ἄλλοι.

αὐτουργούς τινας, 'a sort of quacks,' 'independent dabblers,' '*amateurs.*'

6. καὶ πρόσθεν γε, [*playfully*] 'yes, hitherto I have been concealing from you that I could talk very learnedly,' etc. καί with γέ following implies a 'yes'; cf. *Mem.* II. x. 2, IV. ii. 24. For the participial construction, cf. *Mem.* II. iii.

14; and for ἔχειν, 'could,' *Mem.* IV. ii. 12. πολλὰ καὶ σοφά, as at iv. 18 *infra;* the καὶ here is peculiar to the Greek idiom which unlike English coördinates number with attributes of quality.

ὄντα, 'that I am'; predicative participle, indr. disc.

7. ἐπαινοῦντες, 'thanked him for.' —— ἀχθόμενος, 'hurt,' 'disappointed'; predic. part. of indr. disc., in a subject relation.

αὐτῷ – παρῆλθον, 'assembled at his table.' The bath would be very refreshing after their long dusty walk. They may have gone to a public bath, though more likely they were shown into dressing-rooms at Callias' house. In Plato's *Symp.* Socrates astonishes his friend, as he emerges from the baths in holiday attire and with fashionable half-shoes on his usually shoeless feet: S. explains 'he is dressed up fine to go to a fine man's house' (ἵνα καλὸς παρὰ καλὸν ἴω).

8. οἱ δ' ἄλλοι, κ. τ. λ., 'while the rest, as was nat-ural, reclined': really intended to emphasize the propriety of the boy's sitting, according to Greek etiquette. Schnei-der, indeed, puts ὥσπερ εἰκὸς before οἱ δ' ἄλλοι. Less likely does it refer to the order of the guests.

The couches were arranged on three sides of a rectangle, like a letter ⊓, the open end toward the door. Beginning here, the right-hand side was called the 'first' or 'highest,' the top the 'second' or 'middle,' the left the 'third' or 'lowest' bed. They rested on their left side, and lay usu-ally two on each separate couch in the series. The host's place was in the centre of the middle course; the place of honor among the Greeks was at his left, the next honorable place at his right, and so on alternately. Sometimes the host designated the places, sometimes left it to the instinct of the guests, at other times dispensed with all ceremony and distinctions. Plutarch tells of a pompous man who came late, and finding, as he declared, no place worthy of him untaken, turned on his heel and left amid the guffaws of the already jolly company. At Plato's Symp. they sit according to tastes and friendships, Socrates and the host incidentally occupying the very lowest couch. Xenophon has the place of honor at Seuthes' feast, *Anab*. VII. iii. 29. The parable in Luke xiv. 7–11 is founded on these customs.

If ὥσπερ εἰκὸς does refer to the arrangement, Xenophon would represent his guests as too sensible to be over-particular, and as taking their places perhaps partly according to rule and partly as tastes inclined. It may be assumed that Xen. conceived his guests in some definite disposition. What this was cannot be fixed with certainty; but the following order answers well the conditions of the subsequent conversations, and is as likely as any : Callias in his proper place, Niceratus next him ; then to one side, Lycon and Autolycus, Antisthenes and Socrates; to the other, Critobulus and Charmides, Hermogenes, Philip.

3   11. ἐπιτεταγμένον, 'were enjoined.' G. 1570, 1576; H. 974, 978. *a*. — τῷ ὑπακούσαντι, i.e., the θυρωρός, or 'porter.'

κατάγεσθαι, 'be admitted.' Philip sends in a specimen joke. Banquets were common at which each guest contributed a share of the substantials, and this was brought along in a basket by a slave. Philip declares, playing on the words συνεσκευασμ. and πιέζεσθαι, that 'he has come all prepared — to dine off another's ; and his slave is bent double with carrying — *nothing*, and from having had no breakfast.'

12. ὦ ἄνδρες, 'gentlemen.' —— σκῶμμα: Callias' own repartee. 'Well, as he has brought his provisions along, it were too bad to deny him shelter and a seat. Let him come in and eat them.' Not a happy arrangement for Philip ; what he brings in the way of "provision" is ample enough, but lacks variety — *a hungry belly.*

13. ὁ δὲ, 'and Philip'; the article with δέ used pronominally, always with change of verbal subject. Philip

entered through the hall-way into the αὐλή, an open interior court about which, thus forming a hollow square, were the variously sized apartments, ἀνδρῶνες. Lucian describes a similar intrusion, *Symp.* 12.

προθύμως, 'without any hesitation.'

ἄκλητον. It was not unusual, it appears, for a guest to take a friend along, as Socrates does Aristodemus in Pl. *Symp.* 174 B C.; but that description plainly shows that it was a matter of some delicacy. The host takes pains to set Aristodemus at his ease.

σπουδῆς, 'seriousness.' —— γελ. - ἐνδεέστ., 'rather need a laugh.'

14. δή, the confidential particle in conversation or vivid narrative; like our 'don't you see?' 'you know,' 'you understand,' etc. —— ἀχθεσθείς, 'terribly bored.'

15. ἀναστενάξ. εἶπε, 'groaned out.' —— ἔρρει τὰ ἐμὰ 4 πράγμ., 'my occupation is gone.' ἔρρω, used commonly in a bad sense, 'gone to the dogs.' —— εὐφραίν. οἱ συνόντες, 'the guests might enjoy themselves.' —— ὡς ἀντικληθ., 'with the expectation of being invited in return.'

δεῖπνον εἰσφέρεσθαι : see on § 11 above.

ἀπεμύττετο, 'wiped his face.' —— κλαίειν ἐφαίν., 'appeared to be crying': for difference of κλαίων ἐφαίν., cf. H. 986; G. 1592. 1.

16. παρεμυθ., 'tried to console.' —— ὡς αὖθις, 'promising that another time.'

τῇ ψυχῇ παρακελ. He comically apostrophizes to his soul: 'take heart,' etc. Cf. *Cyrop.* I. iv. 13. So Odysseus in *Od.* v. 17 :

στῆθος δὲ πλήξας κραδίην ἠνίπαπε μύθῳ ·
Τέτλαθι δή, κραδίη · καὶ κύντερον ἄλλο ποτ' ἔτλης.

συμβολαί, then, may be 'engagements' on the field of war, or behind a dinner plate. This was the term for contributions to a feast ; here it is 'banquets.'

CHAPTER II.

5   1. ἔσπεισαν, κ. τ. λ. The removal of the eatables is
followed by the usual ceremonies. To each guest is handed
a wreath, commonly of myrtle, — not mentioned here ; a
libation of undiluted wine is offered to the 'good genius,'
ἀγαθοῦ δαίμονος, each guest sipping a little ; a song is sung
to Apollo, — and then amusements are introduced, and the
πότος proper begins. The first cup is drained to Ζεὺς Σωτήρ.
See Diod. S. IV. iii. 4. Cf. Pl. *Symp.* 176 A.

Xenophon gives no particulars regarding the dishes.
This would not be in good taste ; his guests are men of
refinement. Cf. the caution, ὅπως . . . ἡδυπαθεῖν, at iv. 8
infra. Fish of all kinds were accounted a great delicacy,
especially Copaic eels. Athenæus gives a mass of ill-
digested information on this subject. See Xenophanes' fine
picture of a banquet, *Eleg.* frag. 1.

Συρακόσιος. This stroller was doubtless attracted to
Athens by the Panathenæa. —— τῶν . . . ποιεῖν, 'one of
those able to perform wonderful feats.' —— ταῦτα, i.e.,
'these performances' ; according to others, sc. παιδία.

ὡς ἐν θαύματι, 'in public spectacle,' 'as a show.'

2. ἱκαν. εὐφραίν., 'give great pleasure.' —— τελέως . . .
ἑστιᾷς, 'you entertain us right royally.' It was considered
polite thus to flatter the host on his house, or his furniture,
the dishes, the wines, etc. —— ἄμεμπτον, 'faultless,' 'per-
fect,' 'fine.' —— θεάμ. κ. ἀκροάμ., 'pleasures for the eye
and ear.'

3. τί οὖν εἰ, 'suppose then.'

μηδαμῶς, 'I beg you not.'

μύρου . . . προσδέονται, 'what need have they of perfumery ?' Socrates is objecting to the use of perfumery by
men as effeminate, and he playfully argues : 'it cannot be

that men use perfume for men's sake ; and the ladies, to
whom it is proper and usual, have enough of it themselves,
especially if they have recently gone through the bridal ceremonies ; now what they appreciate most in men is that odor
which betokens physical vigor and devotion to manly pur-
suits.' Cf. Aristoph. *Plutus*, 529 :

. . . μύροισιν μυρίσαι στακτοῖς, ὁπόταν νύμφην ἀγάγησθον.

ἐλαίου : used to anoint the body, lubricating the muscles 6
for athletic exercises.

4. **ἐπιτηδευμ.**, 'training,' 'practice.' —— **πρῶτον**, 'as the
first essential.' —— **ἂν εἴη**, 'would pertain.' 1328 G.; H.
872. —— **τίνος** : G. 1107.

καλοκἀγαθίας, 'noble manhood,' ' virtue ' ; the abstract
from **καλο-κἀγαθός**, for which see on § 1.

χρῖμα, ' unguent.'

Θέογνις, a Dorian of Megara, 540 B.C. The 1400 elegiac
verses which bear his name may be a somewhat later com-
pilation of extracts from his poems ; they consist mainly of
moral aphorisms. His writings were very popular, and a
standard authority on morals. This same couplet (vv. 35–6)
is given to Socrates in *Mem.* I. ii. 20, and by Plato, *Meno*
95 D. For the rhythm, G. 1670; H. 1101.

5. **χρῆταί** γε, 'applies it,' 'acts upon it,' i.e., uses this
moral prescription. —— **ἐβούλετο**, ' had the ambition.'

σὺν σοὶ σκεψ.* αὖ, κ. τ. λ., 'with your help he will
look about, and now again whatever person appears to be
most competent,' etc. : a clear enough sense. Weiske, however, followed by the editors generally, believed there is a
lacuna at the asterisk ; and for this Cobet suggests : τοῦτο
κατέπραξεν, ὅταν δὲ καλὸς κἀγαθὸς γενέσθαι ἐπιθυμῇ, πρὸς
ἑαυτὸν σκεψάμενος.

εἰς τὸ τ. ἐπιτηδ., i.e., for giving a moral training.

6. **τοῦτο**, i.e., morals.

7. **ἀμφίλογον**, 'a matter for debate.' Noticeable through- 7
out is Socrates' skill in obviating or calming disputes.

Epictetus observed and admired this, — *Diss*. IV. v. 3 ;
see also III. xvi. 5.

ἀποτελῶμεν, 'fulfil,' carry out the program, hence here
'attend to.' —— ἐφεστηκυῖαν, 'has come forward.'

8. ἡ δὲ λαμβ., κ.τ.λ. The flute gives the girl her time ;
and she is represented as dancing some figure while keeping
twelve hoops in air.

9. ἐν πολλ.–κ. ἄλλ.–καὶ ἐν οἷς, 'in many other ways and
especially,' etc. Cf. *Œcon*. x. 1. —— γνώμης, 'judgment.'
—— θαρρῶν, 'with assurance.' —— βούλοιτ', κ. τ. λ., 'would
have her know.'

Woman held a very lowly position in Greek social life.
From tender years she was immured in the confinement of
the *gynæconitis*, seeing no strangers, and receiving no edu-
cation beyond that knowledge of housewifery which the
mother might impart. It is a woman herself who says
(Eurip. *Iph. Aul.* 1394) εἷς γ' ἀνὴρ κρείσσων γυναικῶν
μυρίων. Plato speaks of women as γένος εἰθισμένον δεδυκὸς
καὶ σκοτεινὸν ζῆν. And Thucydides makes Pericles say,
'That woman is best who is least spoken of among men,
whether for good or for evil.' Plato in his *Republic* puts
forward more advanced notions, and would subject women
to the same training and the same public duties as men.
The naïve account of the early intercourse between the
young newly-married couple in Xen. *Œcon*. vii–x. is especially interesting.

10. οὕτω γιγνώσκων, 'holding that doctrine.' γιγνώσκειν with adverbs or cognate neuters means 'have an
idea,' 'opinion,' 'belief,' etc.

Ξανθίππην : whose name has ever since been a synonym
for 'shrew.' For other reference to her unpleasant disposition, see *Mem.* II. ii., where Socrates would inculcate upon
his eldest son, Lamprocles, respect for his mother. Xan-
thippe appears to have been a score of years younger than
Socrates.

χρῆ, 'live with.' —— εὐπειθ., 'manageable' ; θυμοειδ.,

'high-spirited.' —— χρῆσθαι κ. ὁμιλεῖν, 'mingle and deal 8 with.' —— οὐκ ἄπο τ. σκοποῦ, 'not wide of the mark,' i.e. 'not inaptly' : ἄπο, so accented when having this adverbial force.

11. κύκλος, κ. τ. λ., 'a ring stuck full of upright swords.' ταῦτα διεπράττετο, 'went through the performance.'

12. ἀντιλέξειν, 'raise the objection.' —— ὡς, declarative, *quotes*, or states a proposition with formality.

ἀνδρεία διδακτόν : for discussion of this debatable question, see *Mem.* III. ix. 1–3. —— ἵεται, 'flings herself.'

13. κράτιστον, 'an excellent idea' ; sc. ἂν εἴη.

ἐπιδείξ. – εἰπεῖν, 'to exhibit — and propose.'

ὁμόσε – ἰέναι, 'to come to close quarters with,' 'to face.'

14. ἡδέως ἂν θεώμην, 'I should be delighted to see.'

Πείσανδρον. The comedians too got after this man for his notorious cowardice ; thus Aristophanes, in *Peace* 395, ironically makes him typical of the war party :

> Πεισάνδρου . . . τοὺς λόφους καὶ τὰς ὀφρῦς.

'The tossing crest and the eyebrows of Pisander.'

In the *Birds*, 1553 *sqq.*, is depicted a shadowy lake, on whose borders Socrates is still 'spirit-leading' as in life, but now in a more literal sense. Hither comes Pisander to reclaim his soul, *which had deserted him in life.*

> πρὸς δὲ τοῖς Σκιάποσιν λί-
> μνη τις ἔστ', ἄλουτος οὗ
> ψυχαγωγεῖ Σωκράτης·
> ἔνθα καὶ Πείσανδρος ἦλθε
> δεόμενος ψυχὴν ἰδεῖν, ἣ
> ζῶντ' ἐκεῖνον προὔλιπε, κ.τ.λ.

συστρατεύεσθαι, 'enlist.' Cf. Ar. *Clouds* 692.

15. ὡς – ἔτι καλλίων, 'how much handsomer.' 9

σχήμασιν, 'steps,' 'graceful movements' : in strict use, 'attitudes.' Plutarch (*Symposiacs* IX. xv. ii. 3) distinguishes three elements : φορά, 'motion,' σχῆμα, '*pose*,' and δεῖξις, 'gesture.'

16. ἀργὸν, 'idle,' 'inactive.' —— ὥσπερ, 'seeming to indicate.' —— εὐφορῶτ., 'more supple,' 'graceful.'

The Greeks carried the art of dancing to remarkable perfection, both in the elegance and the variety of their dances. Especially notable were their mimetic dances. They were adepts in using *motion* to express *emotion*: by features and attitude and bodily movements they represented inward thought and feelings; and thus they acted in panto-mime little dramas, founded mainly on familiar myths, with overpowering effect. Such is the ballet in Ch. ix. *infra*; cf. also vi. 4. See Lucian, *de Saltat.*; Plato, *Laws* 814 D ff.

17. μάλα ἐσπουδ., κ. τ. λ., 'said with perfectly sober countenance, "You laughing at me? Is it because," etc.'

ὑγιαίνειν, 'enjoy better health.' —— ἐπιθυμῶ, 'seek,' 'resort to.' —— μὴ, 'that I may not as,' etc. As in English a verb is suggested from the simile, which would correspond to ποιεῖν.

The course called δολιχός consisted of a number of turns about the stadium, amounting to from 1 to 3 miles.

παχύνονται, 'develop': παχύνειν is 'to make παχύς.' All adjs. in -ύς give rise to similar -ύνω causatives.

ἰσόρροπον, 'well-balanced,' 'symmetrical.'

18. ἐπ' ἐκείνῳ, 'at that thought.' —— συγγυμν., 'partner,' 'companion.'

10 οἶκος ἑπτάκλινος, 'a seven-couched apartment.' The varying sizes of the chambers, or ἀνδρῶνες, opening on the court, were loosely described by the number of couches they would hold. Cf. Athen. II. xxix.

ἐνιδρῶσαι, 'start the perspiration.'

19. μεῖζω . . . γαστέρα, 'a corporation unbecomingly large,' 'excessive *embonpoint*.' —— οὑτοσί, 'here'; the deictic ῑ. G. 412; H. 274. —— ὀρχούμενον: G. 1582.

ἐξεπλάγην, 'was thunderstruck.'

μαίνοιο, 'were gone crazy.'

ἐχειρονόμουν, 'went through an arm exercise.' The term is used specifically of the part played by the arms in mimetic dancing; but also, as here, of calisthenic drill.   See *Chiro-nomia*, Rich's Dict. Antiq.

20.   Philip jestingly compliments Charmides on the happy results of this exercise of his.

ἰσοφόρα, 'equal in weight,' with punning allusion to ἰσόρροπον of § 17, 'symmetrical.'

τ. ἀγορανόμοις, 'before the supervisors of the market.' The ἀγορανόμοι, like the ædiles at Rome, had oversight of the markets, and of buying and selling therein; for violation of regulations they had power to inflict fines upon citizens, and chastisement upon foreigners.   There were five for Athens, and five in the Piræus.

ἀφιστῴης, 'weigh out'; a pres. opt. fr. ἀφιστάω; a late compound, hence dubious here.   Schenkl alters to τις ἀγο-ρανόμος ἀφισταίη σου.

ἀζήμ. ἂν γεν., 'you would escape unfined, you would.' Observe the double ἄν: not uncommon; often for comic effect, as here.   Cf. Ar. *Clouds*, 118, 425, etc.   GMT. 223; and G. 1483. —— ἀντιστοιχῶ, 'be your partner.'

21.   διῆλθε μιμ., 'went through with an imitation of.'

22.   ἀνταπέδειξεν, 'he on the contrary — made appear,' etc. —— σώματος with ὅ τι —— τ. φύσεως, 'than it naturally was.' —— ταῦτα, = διὰ ταῦτα.

τέλος : G. 1060; H. 719.

ἐπάγειν, 'strike up.' —— ἵει, 'jerked about.'

23.   ἀπειρήκει : see ἀπ-εῖπον ; = 'renounce,' 'give up,' 'give out' in general, then especially from exhaustion, and finally 'to be tired out' simply.

φιάλην.   The φιάλη resembled a deep saucer or flaring bowl without either foot or handle, holding anywhere from a pint to a quart or more.   Other common drinking vessels were the κύλιξ, smaller, also saucer-shaped, but having one or two handles on the rim and a foot like that of a wine-glass ; and the ῥυτόν, primitively a literal horn, then devel-oped into various artistic shapes in silver, with ends fash-

ioned into heads of various animals, from the mouths of
which the wine flowed.

24 καὶ ἐμοὶ π. δοκεῖ, 'I too quite approve.'
τῷ ὄντι, 'really.'

μανδραγόρας, a narcotic plant.   Cf. Lucian, *Timon* ii ;
also Demosth. *Phil.* Δ 6 (133.1) : οὐδ' ἀνεγερθῆναι δυνάμεθα,
ἀλλὰ μανδραγόραν πεπωκόσιν ἤ τι φάρμακον ἄλλο τοιοῦτον
ἐοίκαμεν ἀνθρώποις.   The ancients had many superstitious
fancies about this plant ; among others, that it sprang from
human blood.   See Steph. Thesaurus, *sub voc.*   'Popular
etymology' derived its name from ἀνήρ and ἀγορεύω ; and
they believed it uttered cries, when pulled from the ground.

κοιμίζει, 'lulls' ; causative verb, allied to κεῖμαι.

φιλόφροσ., 'mirth.'

Such mirthful laudations of wine have ever found a place
at banquets.   Ebers attributes these to the Egyptians :
"wine is like soap ; it cleanses the soul from sorrow ";
"sorrow is a poison, and wine is the antidote."

25. ταὐτὰ πάσχειν ἅπερ, 'it is with men's bodies just
as with,' etc.   Socrates comically compares men's bodies to
the grain-stalks.   σώματα is read with Schenkl and others
from Athenæus instead of συμπόσια of the Mss.   Dind. and
Sauppe retain the latter, and then alter to τὰ ἐν γῇ φυόμενα.

ἄγαν ἀθρόως, 'too much at once.' —— ποτίζῃ, 'give to
drink' ; causative verb. —— διαπνεῖσθαι, 'be breathed
through,' 'allow the air to circulate' ; this is meant to
parallel ἀναπνεῖν, § 26.

12   καρπογονίαν, 'harvest,' 'maturity.'

26. ἡμῖν : ethical.   H. 770 ; G. 1170. —— σφαλοῦνται
'reel,' 'weaken.'   For the same expression cf. *Cyrop.* I.
iii. 10.

μὴ ὅτι, 'not to mention,' 'much less.'   G. 1504 ; H. 1035.

μικραῖς . . . ἐπιψακ., 'rain upon us with cups small but
frequent.   Cicero makes pleasant allusion to this sentiment,
de Senectute xiv (46) : *pocula delectant me, sicut in Symposio
Xenophontis, minuta atque rorantia.*

ἵνα . . . εἴπω, 'if I may be allowed a Gorgian metaphor.'
For this rhetorician, see on i. 5 *supra*. Callias' use of
κοσμέω in i. 4 smacks somewhat of the school. Longinus,
de Sublim. iii. 2, criticises Gorgias for such *outré* expressions
as Ξέρξης ὁ τῶν Περσῶν Ζεὺς, and γύπες ἔμψυχοι τάφοι.

πρὸς τ. παιγν, 'into a merrier mood.'

Frag. 2 of Critias' Elegiacs is of interest in this connection.

27. περιελαύνοντας, 'driving around.' Philip would
outdo Socrates with a yet bolder metaphor.

It was customary on these occasions to choose a symposiarch, who then fixed the proportion for the wine, and
directed the order and amount of the drinking. For this
post they avoided alike the debauchee and the too sober
man. Plato, like Xenophon, describing the intercourse of
more refined men, dispenses with this official, until late in
the proceedings the tipsy Alcibiades breaks in upon them
and constitutes himself symposiarch.

The Greeks drank no wine undiluted: even half-and-half
(ἴσον ἴσῳ) was looked upon as intoxicating and disreputable.
The usual proportion of water to wine was 3 : 1 or 2 : 1,
more rarely 3 : 2; the first and most common Hesiod
recommends, while at a later date Athenæus speaks of it
contemptuously as fit for frogs (βατράχοις οἰνοχοεῖν). The
supply vessel hence was called κρατήρ, 'mixer.'

CHAPTER III.

1. συνηρμοσμένη, 'tuned in harmony with.' The λύρα
may loosely be said to resemble the modern guitar. The
letter Ψ suggests its outline; it had 3 to 9 strings. The
κιθάρα differed chiefly in the construction of the sounding-
board : κιθαρίζειν applies to both.

τ. ἀφροδίτην, 'passion.'

13

2. **αἰσχρὸν**, sc. ἐστιν; 'is it not a shame?' Plato speaks slightingly of such minstrel amusements for rational men, and in his *Symp.* at once sends the flute-girl off to play by herself or for the women of the house, if she choose. See too his *Protag.* 347 C D.

ἁπτόμενοι, 'engaging in.'

3. **ἀπολάβ. – τ. ὑπόσχ.**, 'get the fulfilment of his promise.' Cf. i. 6. —— **εἰς μέσον φέρ.**, 'contribute.'

μὴ οὐ: G 1551–2; H. 1034. *a*.

4. **μέγιστ. φρονῶ**, 'take most pride.' —— **βαναυσικὴν**, 'mechanical'; conveying too a notion of contempt.

εἰ καλοκἀγ., κ. τ. λ. = 'virtue, if by 'virtue' you mean Rightwisness. Yes, that is the least questionable form of virtue.' The point he proceeds to make is, that while the other popular virtues, Manfulness and Wisdom, may not be absolute goods, there is no variable element in Rightwisness. Cf. *Mem.* IV. ii. 33.

It is proposed to conventionally render **δικαιοσύνη** by 'Rightwisness,' the O. Eng. form of 'righteousness,' which latter is now too specialized, and to discard the misleading and quite inadequate term 'justice.' For the scope of these virtues see author's Introduction to the MEMORABILIA, pp. xviii–xix. —— **ἔστιν ὅτε**; G. 1029; H. 998. *b*.

δοκεῖ: H. 610. *a*, 617. —— **καθ' ἕν**, 'in a single point.'

14   5. **ἐπιμελ. ὅπως**, 'in his anxiety that.' —— **ἀπὸ στόματος**, 'by heart'; 'off the tongue.'

6. **ῥαψῳδοὶ**, the 'rhapsodists,' or professional reciters of the Homeric poems. The same mean opinion of them as a class is expressed in *Mem.* IV. ii. 10; cf. too Plato's *Ion.* The Greeks of Socrates' day had read into these epics whole volumes of ethical wisdom. Homer was to them Bible for theology and morals, and a *vade-mecum* for all practical wisdom as well. It is this underlying inspiration (ὑπόνοια) which the minstrels could not appreciate and expound.

ἀκροώμ. γε, 'hearing them as I do,' etc.: one of the luxuries of a man of wealth.

Στησιμβρότῳ, an interpreter of Homer, mentioned in Plato's *Ion* 530 D. So too, probably, was Anaximander.

7. ἦ οὖν καὶ σύ, = 'do you then mean to say that you,' etc. —— φαῦλος, 'ridiculous.'

8. μηδὲ, sc. εἶναι. The μή negatives are uniformly found with the inf. after ὄμνυμι.

ἐγκονίσ., 'to sand himself in.' After smearing with oil, the athletes covered themselves with sand to afford a better hold. Cf. Plut. *Symposiacs*, IV. *proem.* 7 : αἱ παλαιόντων ἐπιβολαὶ καὶ ἕλξεις κονιορτοῦ δέονται.

9. εὐχαρίστῳ, 'delightful.' —— ἥκ. περιμάχ., 'gives rise to the least contention.'

10. μαστροπείᾳ, 'enticing' ; 'pandering.' An astounding avowal from Socrates.

Καλλιπίδης was a famous tragic actor. He is mentioned by Aristotle, *Poet.* xxvii. 4 : ὡς λίαν γὰρ ὑπερβάλλοντα, πίθηκον ὁ Μυνίσκος τὸν Καλλιπίδην ἐκάλει, — see also *ib.* 7 ; and by Plutarch, see *Apoth. Lac., Ages.* 57, *de Glor. Ath.* vi.

11. ὑποκριτής, first, 'an answerer,' 'one who takes part in dialogue' ; so, 'an actor,' as here : later in a bad sense, 'one who plays a part,' 'hypocrite.'

ὑπερσεμν., 'is excessively vain.' —— πολλ. κλαι. καθίζειν, 'affect an audience to tears.'

12. ἀνερυθριάσας, 'reddening up' : -ιάω is a common termination for verbs expressing a disease or affection of the body ; thus ὠχριάω, 'to be sallow,' ὀφθαλμιάω, 'to have sore eyes,' etc. The Greeks admired and nurtured in their lads this girl-like modesty.

13. φωνήσαντος : GMT. 884. There is no time expressed by this predicative participle, just as in the case of the objective infinitive not in *orat. obl.*

βασιλέως : King with the Greeks meant the Persian monarch. For a similar comparison, see iv. 11 *infra:* also *Cyrop.* VIII. iii. 26.

ἐπ' αὐτοφώρῳ, 'right away,' 'at once' ; the phrase = 'in the very act of theft' ; φώρ is 'thief,' akin to φέρω.

CHAPTER IV.

1. **ἂν εἴη** : see refs. at ii. 4. —— **ἀποδεικνύναι,** 'prove,' 'establish.'

For Callias' boast see iii. 4, *supra*.

ἀπορούντων, 'debating'; 'to be at a loss.'

δίκαιον : translate this and kindred words by 'right,' etc., and not by 'just'; see on iii. 4. So **δικαιοτέρους,** 'better.' —— Cf. *Mem.* IV. iv.

17   2. **ἐλεγκτικῶς,** 'critically,' 'sharply.' —— **τὸ δίκ.,** 'virtue,' say. —— **ὅτου** : G. 1133 ; H. 746. —— **κακουργ. κινδ.,** 'take the risk of committing crime.'

3. **τί δέ,** 'well,' simply ; used to introduce with animation successive elliptical questions.

ἐχθιόνως ἔχουσιν, 'feel more unkindly.' **ἔχειν** with any adverb idiomatically means 'to be,' of a state or condition described by the adverb.

ἅμα . . . αὐτόν, 'at the same time giving him a look which implied that he had him cornered.' The subjective **ὡς** : H. 978 ; G. 1574.

4. **μισθωταῖς,** sc. *οἰκίαις.* —— **ἀνάσχου – ἐλεγχόμ.,** 'allow you to be beaten'; or more strictly, 'allow yourself to be confuted,' i.e. 'give in.'

5. **τὸ ἐπιόν,** 'what is just ahead.'

18   6.   For Niceratus' boast see iii. 5.

πεποίηκε, 'written.' The poet in Homer is **ἀοιδός,** 'the singer,' later he is **ποιητής,** 'the producer.' So 'maker' was used in early Eng. How admiration and the religious instinct had gradually exalted the Homeric poems into an inspired encyclopedia of morals and general wisdom, has already been alluded to ; see on iii. 6. A somewhat analogous process is going on in our day with Shakespeare.

ἦ καὶ βασιλεύειν, κ. τ. λ. : said with a playful malice ;

"king" was a title of abhorrence to the democratic radicals of Athens. The quotation is from *Iliad*, Γ 179; it is quoted by Socrates in *Mem*. III. ii. 2, and is said to have been a favorite verse with Alexander the Great. Observe the *chiasmus*: 'a good prince and a warrior bold.' Niceratus parries the thrust by producing another gem, this vivid picture of the charioteer at the turning-post:

> ' Leaning thy weight some whit to the left on the seat of the chariot,
> That way to sway its course: meanwhile the steed on thy right hand
> Urge with thy goad and thy voice, and cease with the rein to confine
> him.' — HERSCHEL.

This is from *Il.* Ψ 335-7; cited also in Plato's *Ion* 537 A B. See the fine passage describing a similar scene in Sophocles' *Electra* 709 *sqq.*

7. ἐπὶ, sc. τραπέζης. —— ὄψον, 'appetizer,' 'relish.' The quotation is from *Il.* Λ 630, where onions are put upon the table as an accompaniment to a mixed drink. The onion was in high esteem with the ancients as an article of diet. The Greeks got their finest from Cyprus.

πιεῖσθε: πιοῦμαι is a late and rare future for πίομαι; due perhaps to the extension of a false analogy.

8. Νικήρατος: lately married; see on ii. 3.

μὴ διανοηθ., κ. τ. λ., 'that no one could have had the slightest idea of kissing him.' Aristophanes imputes this same device to Attic women, *Thesm.* 493-6.

προσλαβεῖν, 'incur.' —— ὄντως, 'in the truest sense.'

ὅπως μὴ, 'beware lest': G. 1352-4; GMT. 271-3.

ἡδυπαθεῖν, 'to indulge our appetites merely.'

9. ὑποτρώγειν, 'nibble,' 'munch': ὑπο- has here its diminutive notion with verbs; so ὑπογελάω is 'to smile.'

σιτίσ. συμβ., 'feed them — before matching them' Cf. Aristoph. *Achar.* 166 ; also *Knights* 493-4 : [CHORUS *to the belligerent sausage-seller, to prime him for his approaching war of words on the floor of the senate.*]

> Χ. ἔχε νυν, ἐπέγκαμψον λαβὼν ταδί. Α. τί δαί ;
> Χ. ἵν' ἄμεινον, ὦ τᾶν ἐσκοροδισμένος μάχῃ.

Schenkl after Cobet alters σκόρ. σιτίσ. to σκοροδίσαντες :
gratuitously ; one might about as well alter ἀνατείνειν χεῖρας
to χειροτονεῖν in Xen. *passim*.

The Greeks were fond also of quail-fighting.

φιλήσομεν, 'kiss'; translate 'for love-making rather
than for war.'

10. See iii. 7.

δίκην ὑπέχ., 'give an account of'; a legal phrase, 'be
liable to action.' For the Gen., G. 1121 ; H. 745.

οὐδ. ὀρκίζ., 'under no constraint.'

11. τὰ αὐτὰ – πάσχ., 'feel the same attraction tow-
ards.' —— μὴ, see on μηδὲ iii. 8. —— βασιλέως, see on iii. 13.

12. Κλεινίαν. Plato mentions two of this name, to
either of whom this might refer : one — the right one probably — a first cousin, the other a younger brother of Alcibiades, who was himself noted no less for his personal
beauty than for his profligacy. In *Mem.* I. iii. 8, Critobulus'
favorite is represented as a *son* of Alcibiades. A. is known
to have had a son named after himself; if he had one, as
would be natural, named Cleinias from the grandfather,
either this picture is anachronistic, or the reference in the
Mem. must be to a different and later attachment.

From this discussion (§§ 10–20) some idea may be formed
of the extravagant passion for beauty among the Greeks,
one of their most marked traits. How this gave rise to
strong romantic attachments among men, can be better
understood when it is remembered that under their social
system woman led a rigidly secluded life, receiving no culture and knowing no social intercourse whatever. Phidias'
statue of Aphrodite Urania stood upon a tortoise, thus
symbolizing woman's life. See on ii. 9. Herodotus (V. 47)
tells us that the Egestæans in Sicily offered sacrifices as to a
deified hero at the tomb of a man who had been of remarkable beauty. It is related also of men engaged in stripping
the bodies of the slain on a battle-field, that, turning up a

Especially, read the fine passage in Xenophon's *Hiero*
(vi. 1–8), which contrasts with the happy lot of the private
person the fears and burdens of the crowned head.

30. αὐτόν . . . ἐργάς., 'do me some personal violence.'
ἐθεράπευον, 'conciliate;' 'keep on good terms with.'
The sycophants were a class of informers addicted to levy-
ing blackmail even on innocent persons. Cf. *Mem.* II. ix ;
also Demosth. *Aristog.* A. 51–2 (786) for a scorching description of the sycophant.

δαπανᾶν ὑ. τ. πόλεως. Citizens of wealth were expected
to expend large sums in various forms of public service,
called *liturgies ;* such as training a chorus for the theatre,
equipping a troop of soldiers, fitting out a war trireme, etc.
It was not safe to shirk this by going abroad. Cf. *Oec.* ii. 6.

31. τ. ὑπερορίων, 'possessions beyond the boundaries,'
i. e., estates out of Attica, as in the islands. This was
occasioned by the reverses of the Peloponnesian war, which
also prevented farming in Attica. Cf. with this *Mem.* II.
vii. 2.

τὰ ἐκ τ. οἰκίας, 'furniture,' 'chattels.'
πέπραται, fr. πιπράσκω.

32. φόρον, 'tax'; 'contribution.' So τέλος is likewise 'tax,' 'expense,' fr. √ταλ, 'lift,' 'bear,' cf. Lat. *tol-lo,
tul-i ;* entirely distinct from τέλος, 'end.'

The state paid her officials — and every citizen of proper
age was practically an official, legislative or judicial —
a regular fee. The juryman's 3 obols *per diem* would easily
support a poor man. On festival occasions a small sum *per
capita* was distributed to the poorer classes, nominally as
theatre money. There was a poor-fund also.

οὐκέτι οὐδὲν – οὐδενί. A similar emphatic heaping up 23
of negatives was common in early English ; thus Chaucer
(Prol. *C. T.*, 70–1),

> 'He *nevere* yit *no* vileinye *ne* sayde
> In al his lyf unto *no* maner wight.'

So in provincial English: Lowell, *Biglow Papers*, 1st ser., vii.,

> 'Nor I haint never signed no pledge.'

The analytic tendency in language and the principle of economy have abolished this pleonasm.

33. τ. ἀποτροπαίοις, 'the averting deities,' especially Zeus and Apollo; cf. Lat. *Dii averrunci*. See Aristoph. *Birds*, 61.

μάλα φ. ὑπομένω, 'am very ready to accept the risk.'

34. See iii. 8. —— Cf. Cicero, *Paradox.* VI: *animus hominis dives, non arca appellari solet,* — *ib.* i. (44.)

35. ἰδιώτας, 'men in private life.' -της denotes 'agent,' or 'actor in a certain sphere': the denominatives are paroxytone, as αὐλήτης, 'a domestic,' from αὐλή; the verbals with long penult are usually oxytone, as αὐλητής, 'a flute-player,' fr. αὐλέω, — with short penult they are usually proparoxytone.

περιττ. τ. δαπ., 'surplus beyond expenses.'

36. δεινότερα, see on ταῦτα § 19, *supra*. —— τ. ἀπορωτ., 'the most poverty-stricken.' —— Cf. *Mem.* IV. ii. 38.

37. καὶ – οἰκτείρω, 'I do pity.' —— ὥσπερ εἴ τις, 'the case of one who,' etc. —— πολλὰ ἔχω, ironically, as μόλις . . . εὑρίσκω shows. —— ὅμως, κ. τ. λ., 'however, I have enough — to satisfy,' etc. —— ἔξω, 'out of doors.'

ῥιγῶν, infinitive. G. 497; H. 412. *a.*

38. μοι δοκ. εἶναι, 'I think of — as,' etc.

ἀρκοῦσαν, 'satisfactory.'

39. ποιῶν ἐκ. αὐτῶν, 'in the experience of each of these pleasures.' —— τ. συμφέροντος, 'than for my good.'

40. ἐκεῖνο, 'that consideration.' ἐκεῖνος, as οὗτος and similar remote demonstratives, usually refers to something preceding; referring to something following, they impart to it an emphatic prominence. —— φαῦλον, 'menial.'

41. ἡδυπαθῆσαι, 'regale myself.' —— τίμια, 'delicacies.'

πολυτελῆ, 'beyond my means'; fr. πολύς and τέλος, 'expense,' cf. on τέλος at § 32.

ἐκ τ. ψυχῆς ταμ., 'I draw on my mental stores'; others, 'on my appetite,' comparing *Mem.* II. i. 30, and what immediately follows here. But the term should be taken in the same sense throughout the whole episode; cf. § 34 and § 43. Nor is a pun intended. He simply reckons his power to control and use appetite among his varied mental resources.

πλεῖον διαφέρει, 'far ahead in the matter of pleasure.' It seems preferable to regard this as an emphatic double comparative, or else as stating the relative differences of the two courses from the ordinary, rather than here arbitrarily render διαφέρειν 'conduce.'

Θασίῳ. The Thasian, the Chian, and the Lesbian, were among the most famous brands of wine with the Greeks, named from the islands which produced them. Cf. Ath. I. li. *sqq.*

42. εὐτέλειαν, 'cheapness'; see on πολυτελῆ § 41.

43. ἀριθμῷ – σταθμῷ, 'by weight or measure.'

ἐπήρκει, 'dispensed.' —— μεταδίδωμι, 'offer to share'; note the tentative force of the pres. and impf. of δίδωμι and its compounds.

44. ἁβρότατον, 'delicate,' hence 'exquisite.'

Σωκρ. σχολάζων συνδιημ.: for the principle of this nom. case, due perhaps to the τιμῶμαι, cf. G. 927; H. 940; Jelf ii, 673.3.

The Greeks set a high value on leisure (σχολή), — freedom from the cares and responsibilities of public life and from the menial drudgery of business. Socrates jokes on his own ἀπραγμοσύνη, *Mem.* III. xi. 16; and *ib.* ix. 9, seeks to distinguish 'leisure' from 'idleness.' Cf. Ar. *Clouds*, 1007.

For Antisthenes' attachment to Socrates, cf. *Mem.* III. xi. 17; also *Symp.* viii. 4, where to Antisthenes, whose philosophy required the renunciation of pleasures and passions,

Socrates playfully says : Σὺ δὲ μόνος, ὦ Ἀντίσθενες, οὐδενὸς ἐρᾷς; Ναὶ μὰ τοὺς θεούς, εἶπεν ἐκεῖνος, καὶ σφόδρα γε σοῦ.

οἳ . . . ἀρέσκωσι, κ. τ. λ. Socrates loved to be free to choose his companions : cf. *Mem.* I. vi. 5, ii. 6.

26 45. τὸ μηδενὸς προσδεῖσθαι, 'the grace of contentment.' The quotation is from *Il.* I 122-3, 264-5, in the enumeration of a princely gift.—— σταθμῷ κ. ἀριθμῷ : Niceratus quotes this from § 43, there spoken contemptuously ; here as much as to say, 'this filthy lucre.'—— καὶ φιλοχρημ., 'rather too fond of money.'

46. See iii. 14.

47. εὔδηλον, sc. ἐστίν, to which the entire ὡς proposition is subject. The sentiments advanced in this discussion can be paralleled indefinitely in Xen.: for instance, *Mem.* I. i. 19, iii. 2-4, iv. 15-19, IV. iii. 16-17 ; and notably *Hipparch.* ix. 8-9.

27 48. οὔπ. λήθω αὐτούς. Cf. Epict. *Diss.* I. xiv. 13-4: ὥσθ', ὅταν κλείσητε τὰς θύρας, καὶ σκότος ἔνδον ποιήσητε, μέμνησθε μηδέποτε λέγειν ὅτι μόνοι ἐστέ · οὐ γὰρ ἐστέ · ἀλλ' ὁ θεὸς ἔνδον ἐστί, καὶ ὁ ὑμέτερος δαίμων ἐστί · καὶ τίς τούτοις χρεία φωτὸς εἰς τὸ βλέπειν τί ποιεῖτε ;

φήμας, κ. τ. λ.: cf. *Mem.* I. i. 3 ; *Cyrop.* VIII. vii. 3 ; also Aesch. *Prom.* 484-499. φῆμαι were utterances of men to which an ominous sense might be attached at will : well illustrated by Cicero's fruit-seller's cry, *Cauneas* (Caunian figs), which suggested *cav' ne eas* ('beware of going'). *De Div.* II. xl. (84). So οἰωνοὺς refers to the flight and notes of birds as a means of augury.

49. ἄπιστον, 'incredible.'
εὐφημῶ, 'speak reverently.'

28 50. ὅταν – ἀγαθ. ἔχ. 'when prosperous.'—— ταῦτα, sc. δεῖπνα or συμπόσια.

ἀμεταστρεπτί, 'precipitately'; 'without turning round.'

51. Niceratus complains that his experience is just the

reverse; and the effect is heightened by his self-confessed stinginess, cf. § 45.

οἵ - ἂν, 'those who' : G. 1431. 1 ; H. 914. B.

γενεαλ. τ. συγγ., 'hunt up the relationship.'

52. διαφθεῖραι, 'corrupt.'

55. νευρόσπαστα, 'puppet-shows' ; 'pulled by string.' ταῦτα γάρ, 'why, that's the reason,' etc. ; sc. διά. He puns on ἀφθονίαν – ἀφορίαν : perhaps 'a mine of luck, but a minus of brains,' may be allowed us.

56. See iii. 10. —— ἀδόξῳ, 'disreputable.'

ὅσα . . . ἀποκρίν.: there is a hit at this characteristic method of Socrates in Ar. *Clouds*, 345.

πάνυ μὲν οὖν is 'certainly' ; one of the commonest phrases for assent.

57. μαστροποῦ, 'a go-between'. —— ἣν ἂν ἢ ὃν ἂν μα- στρ., 'the person whom he entices' ; 'him or her,' etc.

ἐν - τι – εἰς τ. ἀρέσκ., 'one element in pleasing.'

58. ἔστιν, 'it is possible.' —— τί δέ, simply 'well' ; an idiomatic transitional phrase in a series of questions.

οἱ π. φιλ. ἀγ., 'which conciliate.'

59. ἐσχίσθησαν. The answer 'certainly' comes so mechanically in time that Xen. comically represents some as failing to observe that this last is no longer a leading question.

60. ἀρέσκοντας, pred. object ; sc. ἀνθρώπους, the pri- mary.

61. After partially developing the innocent significance — however questionable the propriety — of his remarkable metaphor, Socrates waggishly ascribes the offensive epithet and trade to Antisthenes, much to the latter's disgust.

τ. ἀκόλουθον, 'sister art.' —— εἰργασμ. : 'accomplished.' προαγωγείαν, 'the procurer's art.'

62. εἰργασμένῳ : G. 1588. —— προαγωγ., 'enticed away.' ἐρῶντα, 'had a passion for.'

Προδίκῳ : see on i. 5 ; and recall Prodicus' favorite maxim

there quoted. Hippias also was a famous Sophist and rhetorician, very versatile and accomplished. See Socrates' dialogue with him, *Mem.* IV. iv.

τὸ μνημονικὸν. On mnemonics *loci classici* are Cic. *de Orat.* II. lxxxvi–lxxxviii.; *ad Herenn.* III. xvi. *sqq.*; Quintil. XI. ii. 11 *sqq.*

31 63. Ἡρακλεώτην, 'of Heraclea'; probably Zeuxippus, a painter; cf. Pl. *Protag.* 318 B.

Αἰσχύλον, not the tragic poet, who was long dead.

ἐκυνοδρομ., κ. τ. λ., 'went to work and tracked each other down.' κυνοδρομεῖν, 'to run down with dogs,' is comically used to describe their search; for its literal use see *Cyneg.* vi. 17–22.

64. πόλεσι . . . συμμάχοις: so all the Mss., Dind., Sauppe. Various attempts have been made here to improve the concinnity and precision of our author: thus— πόλεσι καὶ ἰδιώταις φίλος καὶ σύμμαχος, Finckh, followed by Schenkl.

ὡς κακῶς ἀκούσας, 'thinking yourself defamed'; with this idiomatic use of ἀκούω, cf. Lat. *bene audire*, etc.

ταῦτα, see at iv. 19. —— σεσαγμένος, 'overwhelmed'; 'loaded down,' fr. σάττω. He had boasted his mental wealth (iv. 34.)

CHAPTER V.

1. See iv. 19–20.
ἀνθίστασαι, 'meet,' 'come to the scratch.'

32 2. εἴ τι ἔχ. σοφόν, 'if you are clever enough.'

μόνον, κ. τ. λ.: Though it would be wittier to give this speech to Socrates, the exactly similar stipulation in § 8 below must be referred to Critobulus, to make most forceful the allusion therein to Antisthenes, Socrates' bosom friend. With προσενεγκ. sc. τίς. Further on some changes in assigning the dialogue of this chapter, it is believed, will commend themselves.

τ. λαμπτῆρα. It seems there was but a single lamp, which could not have made the apartment very light. So in Lucian's *Symp.* (46) upsetting the lamp leaves them in total darkness.

τ. δίκης, with ἀνάκρισιν. Socrates treats this as a regular case in court, and asserts his right to cross-examine the opposing party.

3. With the following discussion compare that in *Mem.* III. viii. 4–7 ; see also IV. vi. 9.

ἀψύχοις, 'inanimate.'

4. εὖ πεφυκότα, 'well-adapted' ; i e. by nature, as εὖ εἰργ. is by man's fashioning.

5. ἀν – εἴησαν : the potential optative puts a conclusion deferentially ; some undefined condition lurks in the mind, such as, 'if we were to apply your admission,' etc. G. 1327, 1329.

διὰ τ. ἐπιπόλ. εἶναι, 'because they stand out so.'

καρκ. εὐοφθαλμ. Crabs belong to the order *Podophthalmia* among crustaceans : their eyes are mounted on flexible stalks, which they can thrust out an inch more or less, and retract at will within the shell. Hence Socrates discerns another excellent feature, *protection*, πρὸς ἰσχὺν, κ. τ. λ. The editors generally have either overlooked or ridiculously misconceived the point of this comparison. One notes that the crab's eyes are compound, a fact which a good microscope alone could have revealed, and not at all a unique feature in the crab. So likewise Schneider informs us that crabs' eyes are "hard" (*duri*).

6. τὸ – σιμὸν, is used abstractly (like τὸ καλὸν), 'snub- **33** ness' ; so τ. ὀρθοῦ : translate generically, 'the snub-nose,' 'the straight one.' Critobulus puts this question, following up his previous one.

ὥσπερ ἐπηρ. διατετείχικε, 'rears, as it were, a beetling

wall between'; the idea seems to be that of a frowning rampart separating belligerents. We may recall the nose of Monsieur Rigaud in Little Dorrit : "a hooked nose, handsome after its kind, but too high between the eyes, by probably just as much as his eyes were too near to one another."

7. διὰ ... φίλημα : Socrates sees another superiority in this same connection.

αἴσχιον : so sighs Critobulus, — if thickness is utility, and utility is beauty.

Ναΐδες : strictly the name of the Nymphs of lake and stream and inland waters. The Satyrs are represented as ardent lovers of the Nymphs. Cf. Ovid, Pont. IV. xvi. 35 ; Naïdas a Satyris caneret Fontanus amatas. See on the Sileni at iv. 19, and on the Nymphs at vii. 5.

8. διαφερόντων is imperative ; δια- in the compound is 'apart,' 'for one side or the other' : 'cast their votes.'

παθεῖν ἢ ἀποτῖσαι, was a court formula ; originally, 'a fine or other form of penalty.'

μόνον, κ. τ. λ. : for Antisth. cf. iv. 44 and note ; 34 sqq., 64.

κρυφῇ, i. e., improvising a ballot-box (καδίσκος), instead of laying their votes openly upon the table as by the other method, — φανερὰν τὴν ψῆφον φέρειν. In voting each person received two ballots, or voting pebbles, of different color ; one he dropped into the voting urn, the other he retained or dropped into a second or storage urn. The regulation urn was fitted with a tube having a funnel-shaped orifice (κημός), into which the hand could be thrust in voting.

9. διέπραττε, 'secured' ; with ἀντιπρ., 'had,' with γενέσθαι, 'had it settled that.'

34 ἀναδήματα, 'tokens of victory' : predicate, and used figuratively ; specifically, 'garlands.'

10. ἐξέπεσον, 'were turned out.' —— πᾶσαι is playful and formal : a unanimous verdict. There were but two ballots cast, of course. The use of plurals throughout is comic. Socrates in δικαστὰς keeps up to the last the illusion of a

court-trial, while he also terms his judges κριταί : in either capacity, as ' umpires' or as ' dicasts,' they have been most shamefully bribed, no less successfully than Paris of old. Some commentators have shown obtuseness in supposing that all the guests voted, which is contrary, moreover, to both spirit and letter of the original proposition, iv. 20.

CHAPTER VI.

1. πείθειν, ' obtain consent of.'

παροινία, use the Greek word, as there seems to be no satisfactory English equivalent : it refers to the humor and conduct of a man under the influence of drink.

2. παρ' οἶνον λυπεῖν, ' being offensive over one's cups.' σιωπῶν. Cf. Simonides' remark to the silent guest : ὦ ἄνθρωπε, εἰ μὲν ἠλίθιος εἶ, σοφὸν πρᾶγμα ποιεῖς · εἰ δὲ σοφός, ἠλίθιον. — Plut. Symposiacs, III, init.

οὐδ' ἂν τρίχα - παρείρειε, ' one could not insert a hair even.' — μὴ ὅτι, as at ii. 26.

3. βούλ. - διαλέγωμαι : G. 1358 ; H. 866. 3. b.

Νικόστρατος was a famous actor ; see Plut. Glor. Ath. vi., also Suidas, sub voc.

4. μορφάζοις, ' gesticulate,' ' give the expressions.' For expression by pantomime see on ii. 16.

5. Callias proposes a weak conundrum : the answer, συριγμός, ' whistling,' is applicable to the notes of the pipes or to that hiss which is the instinctive expression of disapproval.

6. φροντιστὴς, may be ' the Thinker,' then ἀφρόντιστος, ' thoughtless,' or ' Reflecter ' and ' unreflecting.' Then if τ. μετεώρων be ' high-flown subjects,' μετεωρότερον may be given ' higher '; or use ' celestial ' simply. It is difficult

to preserve the word-play in translating. Aristophanes in the
Clouds, exhibited but a year or two previous, had dubbed
Socrates ' the phrontist,' and had depicted him as investigat-
ing celestial and physical phenomena, not more to cast re-
proach upon an advancing science suspected of skeptical
tendencies, than by an absurd literalization of metaphor to
characterize the philosophical spirit of the day as vapory
and visionary. The ordinary spectator like the Syracusan
would appreciate the formal aspect only.

36   7. ἄνω ... ὄντων : the emendation of Madvig, adopted
by Schenkl, for ἀνωφελεστάτων of the Mss. Socrates follows
this up with a pun still more audacious.

ψυχρά, 'flat'; or 'frigid,' as the Greeks termed a poor
joke. Socrates alludes to his puns.

8. πόσους ψύλλης, κ. τ. λ. The fellow becomes abu-
sive, and quotes some of the scurrility of the *Clouds :* where
(144–152) Socrates is made to devise a clever means of cal-
culating the parabola of a flea's jump *in flea's feet.*

κηρὸν διατήξας, εἶτα τὴν ψύλλαν λαβὼν
ἐνέβαψεν εἰς τὸν κηρὸν αὐτῆς τὼ πόδε,
κᾆτα ψυγείσῃ περιέφυσαν Περσικαί.
ταύτας ὑπολύσας ἀνεμέτρει τὸ χωρίον.

The Mss. have ψύλλα and ἀπέχει : which, if correct, would
be intended to represent the fellow as bungling his witti-
cism.

εἰκάζειν, is used both of recognizing and of presenting a
likeness or comparison. Antisthenes suggests to Philip :
' you are a clever clown and mimic ; don't you think the Syracusan's conduct demands a setting down ? ' But Socrates
objects to calling any names, lest P. be like him.

9. πάντ᾽ αὐτοῦ βελτίω, κ. τ. λ., 'make him out every way
better than he is.' This is the reading generally adopted for
βελτίων of the Mss., and the interpretation founded thereon :
i.e., πάντα τὰ ἐν αὐτῷ βελτίω, sc. τῆς φύσεως.

10. ἄξια τ. δείπ. ἐργάσ. : cf. i. 15.

CHAPTER VII.

1. **εἰκάζειν**, 'mimicry,' — which some persisted in having 37 from Philip.

2. **ἦσαν**, for ᾖσεν of the Mss.: Sauppe, Schenkl, after Mosche. Socrates simply led off in the song. Aristoph., *Clouds* 1356, gives the theme of such a song: τὸν Κριόν, ὡς ἐπέχθη, 'Sir Ram, how he was shorn.' The deed of Harmodius and Aristogiton was a favorite subject for these popular drinking songs, or *scolia*. It was usual for the singer to hold a branch of myrtle; this was passed from one to another, who was then expected to take up and continue the song.

τροχὸς τ. κεραμ., 'a potter's wheel.'

ὡς ῥᾷστ. διάγ., 'it may be as easy for,' etc. For ὅπως ἄν, GMT. 351.2, App. iv.

3. **τὸ - θεωρεῖν**, κ. τ. λ. — (sc. ἐστιν) ἥδιον.
διαστρέφ., 'contorting.'

4. **χαλκεῖον**, is the bronze body of the lamp. Ordinary 38 lamps were earthen; the wealthy had bronze and even silver lamps.

ἐ. ταὐτὸν - ἐπισπεύδει, 'promote the same ends,' etc.; 'are not in place.'

5. **Χάριτές**, κ. τ. λ. The *Graces*, goddesses of beauty and refinement, were three, — Euphrosynê, Aglaia, and Thalia. They were sometimes represented draped, and sometimes not; the former in the group accredited to Socrates' chisel which Pausanias saw in the Acropolis. Paus. I. xxii. 8. The *Hours*, goddesses of the seasons and of order, were also three according to Hesiod, — Eunomia, Dikê, Irênê. They were represented as blooming maidens, laden with the products of the seasons. The *Nymphs* were a more numerous class, and of various orders and sub-orders, as Nereids,

Naiads, Oreads, Dryads, etc. They were the goddesses that gave soul and sacredness to natural objects, streams, groves, and the like. On all see Class. Dict. Cf. Hor. *Carm.* I. iv. 6–7 :

> Junctaeque Nymphis Gratiae decentes
> Alterno terram quatiunt pede.

γράφονται, 'are depicted.' —— συνεκροτεῖτο, 'got ready his performance.'

———◦◦———

CHAPTER IX.

39

1. ὥρα ἦν αὐτῷ. Autolycus seems to have been still in training. Day evidently was just breaking, and he goes off to take his morning constitutional. There is art too in thus removing the lad from an exhibition which would be regarded hardly proper for one of his years.

2. ὦ ἄνδρες. The showman speaks a prologue, interpreting the forthcoming ballet.

Ἀριάδνη. Ariadne, according to the legend, was the daughter of Minos, king of Crete ; she helped Theseus to slay the Minotaur, and then eloped with him. Theseus, however, abandoned her on the island Naxos ; whereupon she became the spouse of Dionysus.

ὑποπεπωκὼς, 'who had been taking a little' ; 'rather tipsy' : for ὑπο- see on ὑποτρώγειν iv. 9.

3. ἂν ἔγνω : G. 1337, 1456.

40

4. ἐφίλησεν, 'kissed.' —— αὖθις, '*encore !*'

5. ἀσπαζομένων, 'caressing.'
ἀναπτερωμένοι, 'with no little emotion.'

6. ὥστε ... συνομ. ἂν : G. 1449, 1337.
ἐφειμένοις, 'permitted.'

7. γεγημακότες, Niceratus, Critobulus ; οἱ ὑπομείν., i.e., Antisthenes, Charmides, Hermogenes.

περιπατήσοντες : Socrates' usual habit, see *Mem*. I. i. 10.

Plato's *Symposium* has a more picturesque ending, if one less dignified and proper : the intrusion of a crowd of revellers ; the scene becomes turbulent, and the soberer guests slip away ; cock-crow finds a scattered group, drunken and asleep ; Socrates and Aristophanes with the tragic poet Agathon, the host, alone awake and still passing the bowl ; Socrates pressing upon the others his views that the genius of the tragic and of the comic muse is essentially one, while they nod under it, and one after the other drops off to sleep ; and Socrates quits the field to pass the day in his usual manner.

INDEX.

INDEX

OF

PROPER NAMES AND PRINCIPAL MATTERS.

———◆———

THE references are mainly to chapter and section, and will serve alike for Text and Notes.

LIST OF OMISSIONS.

University Press: John Wilson and Son, Cambridge.

DATE DUE